RIGHT
FOR A
REASON

RIGHT
FOR A
REASON

LIFE, LIBERTY, AND A CRAPLOAD
OF COMMON SENSE

Miriam Weaver and
Amy Jo Clark

SENTINEL

SENTINEL
Published by the Penguin Group
Penguin Group (USA) LLC
375 Hudson Street
New York, New York 10014

USA | Canada | UK | Ireland | Australia | New Zealand | India | South Africa | China
penguin.com
A Penguin Random House Company

First published by Sentinel, a member of Penguin Group (USA) LLC, 2014

Photograph on page 80: Times to Treasure Photography

ISBN 978-1-59523-116-1

Printed in the United States of America
10 9 8 7 6 5 4 3 2 1

Set in Garth Graphic Std
Designed by Alissa Rose Theodor

FOR MR. DAISY AND MR. MOCK

CONTENTS

RIGHT
FOR A
REASON

INTRODUCTION

Hi there.

If you're reading this right now, chances are you're a frustrated conservative. And you've got good reason to be frustrated. If you're like us, you're practically dizzy from how often you've shaken your head at the stupidity of low-information voters who couldn't pick Nancy Pelosi out of a photo lineup but can rattle off the names of every single member of the Kardashian clan. Casting political votes is now on par with casting *American Idol* votes—people care more about the celebrity "it" factor than they do about competence. The result? We're smack-dab in the middle of Obama's "fundamental transformation" of our beloved country, and it's been positively painful.

Maybe you're frustrated that conservatives haven't been able to effectively communicate their ideas in a way that resonates with the public. Maybe you're frustrated that the mainstream media has been complicit in glamorizing the liberal narrative. Maybe you're frustrated because you're not sure you fit in with other conservatives, because you're not the stereotypical stodgy old white dude. Maybe you're frustrated because you're sick of social issues branding conservatism and turning otherwise like-minded people away from it. Or maybe you're just frustrated that we're making all of these assumptions about why you might be frustrated.

Whatever is frustrating you about conservatism, we want you to know something. You're not alone.

Ever since we started our website (chicksontheright.com) back in early 2009, we've been inundated with messages and comments from both liberals and conservatives who cannot wrap their minds around the fact that women like us exist. We're faithful, but irreverent. We're Christians, but we can curse like sailors. We are breadwinners in our families, but we have mad respect and appreciation for women who choose a traditional stay-at-home-mom role. We expect respect and sensitivity from our husbands, but we love them because they're *men*—not metrosexual wusses who use more hair product than we do. We're conservatives, but we love our LGBT friends and don't care whom they sleep with. We're pro-life, but we're also pro–birth control and pro–Plan B.

"How can you vote for Republicans who want to take away women's rights?" liberals shriek. "Don't you know that you're voting against your own gender?" they wail. "Conservatives want to eliminate access to contraception!" they whine. And our favorite: "You bitches need to get back into the kitchen where you belong and make your rich husbands some sandwiches!"

We're not kidding. We get that all the time. That one makes us laugh the hardest.

It's often not much better with folks standing next to us on the right side of the aisle.

"How dare you take the Lord's name in vain?" they holler. "Why must you be so snarky? Change your tone!" they demand. "Why do you wear shorts? Cover up!" they insist. "You're just not conservative *enough* to be conservative," they say.

But here's what we've learned over the past half decade. Despite what the mainstream media wants you to believe, there are thousands and thousands of people out there who are just like us. They are breaking the conservative stereotype by not being old white dudes. They giggle at dirty jokes and are a bit more relaxed about social issues. They're strong willed, fed up, and pissed off, and we're talking to them in a way that resonates. Because we're regular chicks talking to them like regular chicks. Not like pundits, not like politicians, and not like policy-makers, but like *people*. People who live in the real world, who care about the country, care about its future, but who are neither bought nor paid for by some special-interest group. We are not a new breed of conservative—we've just been ignored by the media, and we are sick of it. Fortunately, we happen to be extra loud and persistent. And we don't give a damn about what anyone else thinks about us.

. . . .

Despite what the mainstream media wants you to believe, there are thousands and thousands of people out there who are just like us.

. . . .

If there's anything we've learned over the past five years of being the Chicks on the Right (in addition to being breadwinners, moms, wives, friends, etc.), it's that conservatism is *right*. Our kind of conservatism is rooted in the United States Constitution, which places the power of the people over that of the government. Conservatism is about personal responsibility, economic liberty, free enterprise, and working your butt off in the most exceptional country on the planet. Conservatism, above all else, is about protecting *freedom*. It's not just our political ideology. It's our value system, our attitude, our foundation . . . our *essence*.

And it's right.

We know what you're thinking. You're wondering, "If conservatism is right, Chicks, then why is our country voting so *wrong* these days?"

That's the very question we asked ourselves back in 2008, and answering that question ultimately led to the development of our website. As we watched in horrified awe as Obamamania swept the country, we realized that liberals were succeeding at portraying conservatives unfairly, and they were winning elections because of it. We realized that we didn't want to watch that happen without doing whatever we could to correct the perception. So chicksontheright.com was born, along with our site names, which have stuck ever since: "Mock" and "Daisy." If you are reading this book because you're a fan of our website or our radio show, those are the names you know us by. Now is probably as good a time as any to introduce ourselves to you with our real names: Miriam (Mock) and Amy Jo (Daisy). It's nice to meet you.

We recognized, when we started our site, that conservatism was in dire need of a makeover, particularly in the messaging department. While the GOP can't seem to get its crap together on the Hill, we've been busy reaching out to the real people that they ostensibly serve—conservatives who understand what being on the right is all about, real people who walk the walk every day. And not only have we reached out to them, but we've also listened to them. What they've said is that they are happy to know that there are others in the Chicks on the Right community we've built who get it. They're overjoyed to be among others who are right for a reason. If you're reading this book, then you are officially part of the community building, too.

(Not to be confused with community *organizing*, which is a whole different thing. In fact, if there's someone out there who actually knows what community organizing is, we'd love to hear a definition, along with an explanation about why it has become pretty much the sole prerequisite for becoming the president of the United States.)

But back to the community we've built. (And yes, Mr. President, *we did build that*.) We're delighted to have you on board as we work on the makeover of conservative messaging. Because that's what this country is about, after all: Real people making a real difference. For all the right reasons.

The liberal narrative is too well scripted and too effective to ignore, so in addition to the other channels (like our daily website posts, our drive-time radio show, and regular newspaper column) we use to vent our frustrations, we've decided to codify why we're right with our very own Chicks on the Right manifesto. And that's what you're about to read.

Because listen: It's time to recharge our conservative batteries. It's time for a *real*, humor-filled, snarktastic look at what makes conservatism right. Liberals have the stranglchold on messaging right now, and that's partly because they've perfected the art of making the epic lie of liberalism sound like it's a good thing. We conservatives have truth and rationality and logic on our side. We just need to remind ourselves *why* we're right, and we need that reminder delivered in a way that's not a lecture, not a history lesson, and not a complicated political diatribe.

That's why we've written this book. It's our invitation to you to join the book version of a Chicks on the Right pep rally. It's going to be snarky, and it's going to be fun, so settle in and get ready to feel validated, energized, and ready to carry the conservative message forward to others in a fresh, fun way. Because if you're a conservative, you're *right*. With plenty of good reasons.

CHAPTER 1

Capitalism Is a Good Thing

Remember the hilarious Occupy Wall Street movement? A filthy subset of society who pooped on police cars and smoked a lot of weed in public parks managed to make big waves by furiously decrying "evil corporations" and the "establishment." Those silly, well-intentioned, deeply misguided hippies. Unfortunately, their PR stunt partially worked—it did a number on the public perception of capitalism being a good thing.

Even though Occupy Wall Street's existence was mercifully brief, the movement's absurdity lives on in liberals who espouse the same nonsensical ideas. Progressives believe in the redistribution of wealth—that simply existing entitles them to other people's money. At the same time, they believe that success is a sign of greed and that capitalism—a system that rewards the hard work of an individual—is one of the roots of evil in our country. As a result, they see nothing wrong with punishing success and rewarding failure in the form of taxpayer bailouts. They've redefined poverty in an attempt to even the playing field and make us all equal in a hippie-happy liberal paradise where no one is better, no one is smarter, and—you guessed it—no one is richer or poorer than anyone else. Their arguments are largely based on peace-loving, materialism-shunning, greed-shaming bullshit, and it's important to remember why they are *so freaking wrong.*

Listen up, folks. *Success and the money that comes with it are good things.* It's the drive to succeed that produced money, freeing us from a barter economy and increasing our prosperity. That same drive produced capitalism, a system that has increased the quality of life for millions of people. It's true, money can be used for evil, and yes, capitalism isn't perfect, but as Ayn Rand said, "Wealth is the product of man's capacity to think." And let's face it. The alternatives—poverty and thoughtlessness—really kind of suck.

As young women back in the day, we Chicks couldn't wait to get out on our own and start making money. Making our own way gave us a sense of independence, a sense of accomplishment, and the sense of personal satisfaction that comes with doing something worthwhile and earning something tangible in return. Today we use the money we earn to feed our families, heat our homes, and put clothes on our backs, and we like that money for good reason. Money isn't just good; it's necessary, and that's an inevitable fact of life—one that progressives will never be able to escape, no matter what kind of fundamental transformation they plan for this free-market country of ours. We're right about this.

There's a reason the phrase "the American dream" was coined. It embodies an idea that perfectly fits within conservative ideology—the idea that we are free to work hard to achieve success. While liberals cling like tree sloths to promises of everything being provided to them by the government, conservatives cling to the notion of self-sufficiency. Capitalism is the cornerstone of that self-sufficiency, an economic system that ensures that individual people and businesses own the means of production, not the government. Conservatives take pride in the way capitalism encourages ownership and working hard, while liberals complain that capitalism cuts them off from the government teat. Conservatives want equal opportunity. Liberals want equal outcomes. They fail to realize that equal outcomes mean everyone is equally miserable.

We're capitalists because we'd rather be happy. And blissfully successful. And able to take any extra money we have to buy a killer pair of pumps.

· ·

While liberals cling like tree sloths to promises of everything being provided to them by the government, conservatives cling to the notion of self-sufficiency.

· ·

HIPPIES VS. CAPITALISM

Let's take a look at the Occupy movement a little more closely. To these hippies, capitalism, along with the success it brings, is the root of evil in our country. Shortly after the movement's inception, several of Occupy's more prominent members decided to organize their thoughts into a manifesto of sorts.[1] We Chicks read it when it was in its infancy, and were completely freaked out by what we read. And while we were tempted to say, "Holy wow—look at the insane ramblings of the crazy hippies" and just dismiss it, the reality is that those authors and editors represent perhaps hundreds of thousands of like-minded wackjobs who are oblivious to the fact that their demands, if met, would cause the eventual collapse of our entire country. But hey, whatever, right? It's nothing a little weed can't make better.

THE AMERICAN PEOPLE'S NEW ECONOMIC CHARTER: THE OWS MANIFESTO

Check out these choice nuggets from that masterpiece:

Goldman Sachs, Citibank, Chase, Bank of America, and Wells Fargo, as well as other "larger than life" institutions like them, "need to redirect funds from their profit sheets on a regular basis to community bank start-ups or credit unions to assure economic diversity within the nation to state and county regulations." So basically any small business owner with a dream of growing his or her company to "larger than life" size should be prepared, once they succeed, for their profits to be redirected to smaller, struggling operations in the name of "economic diversity." Because *fairness.*

The whole matter of salary and compensation was completely thought out by the OWS folks. They created "New Salary Range Recommendations Based on Concepts of Economic Sustainability and Right Livelihood." *Behold*—their proposed compensation guidelines:

Bankers $20,000
Lawyers $27,500
Realtors $25,000
Doctors $28,000
Nurses $27,500
Teachers / Librarians / Train engineers / Bridge maintenance /
Ship pilots, etc. $35,000
Police $36,000
Public servants $28,500
Laborers $20,000
Other public sector $30,000
Other private sector $29,000

Technical/Research/Academic $36,000
Entrepreneurs / Business owners $10,000
Congress $30,000
President $40,000
Soldiers N/A
Defense workers $25,000
All jobs include full health benefits for worker and family,
full retirement benefits, full free education for children.

Amazing, isn't it? It completely escaped the OWS folks that entrepreneurs and business owners are the very people who would be footing the bills, and yet they assigned them the smallest salaries. And soldiers? Eh, screw 'em. It's not like they're really doing anything important anyway.

What was ridiculous about the Occupy movement was that the folks least affected by it happened to be the Wall Street bankers. Yeah, it was business as usual for the very people the protesters were protesting. Meanwhile, the people on whose behalf they claimed to be protesting (the "99 percent") suffered the most. Among the complaints were the nonstop drumming, the public urination and filth, and the barricades that blocked access to shops and restaurants along Broadway, disrupting the livelihoods of their owners. One coffee shop had to lay off twenty-one people due to protesters. The owner lamented, "Now, Wall Street is deserted. The only people who walk down Wall Street are people who have to walk down Wall Street. It's transformed from a beautiful pedestrian mall to a police siege."[2]

Way to go, OWS. *Way. To. Go.*

Occubot hippies couldn't even see the painful irony when they held up their iPhones and tweeted "Down with dirty corporations!" So we can't very well expect them to see the stupidity in their ridiculous manifesto that was obviously written with a lot of marijuana, but not reality, as the basis.

The fact that the protesters tweeted against capitalism via their iPhones wasn't the only irony we mocked at the time. Remember all those fancy-shmancy meals that the OWS folks were getting treated to courtesy of some sympathetic restaurants? Well, it turns out that the volunteer kitchen staff was pissed off when they realized homeless people were eating the meals along with the "real" activists. In protest, the volunteers decided to only serve rice instead of the normal organic fancy-food fare. Take *that*, homeless people![3]

OWS demanded that people who had more wealth than they did "pay their fair share" and stop being so greedy, yet they were angry that homeless people who had far less than they did were helping themselves to what the OWS people had, *without earning it.*

The protesters were too ignorant to realize it, of course, but they totally made the 1 percent's point *for* them. It's not much fun when people demand that you give them something when they've done nothing to earn it, is it?

We should remind everyone that many people in President Obama's administration happily endorsed the Occupy movement. In fact, they practically salivated over it. Nancy Pelosi said of the movement, "God bless them for their spontaneity. It's independent, it's young, it's spontaneous, and it's focused. And it's going to be effective." According to Nancy McBotox, the Tea Party is a bunch of racist terrorists, but the hippies pooping in the street?

Total patriots, y'all.

Democrats liked Occupy Wall Street because the hippies and progressives who protested shared their view that government isn't just the foundation of a successful economic system, but its salvation as well. Progressives believe evil corporations are responsible for all the world's problems, and only an all-seeing and all-powerful government can take care of everyone. Which is why bailouts (of those evil corporations!) are a thing now.

BAILOUTS SUCK

Back in 2008 when the word "bailout" became über popular, not only were citizens of this country holding out their hands expecting entitlements, but *companies* were starting to demand the same treatment as well. Bailouts, put simply, are entitlement programs on steroids, and conservatives are right to despise them.

At first, we taxpayers handed around $800 billion to banks and insurance companies, ostensibly to save them (and our economy in the process) from certain doom. But in reality, we simply paid for a bunch of golden parachutes and spa treatments for the worthless executives who helped cause the companies' failures in the first place.

And then came the car companies. Or, if we're being real about this, then came the car company *unions*. The unions were in large part to blame for the fact that GM and Chrysler were in dire straits, but we taxpayers ponied up to cover the generous pensions and health plans of union members. In other words, we were *chumps*.

You know what bailout money does? It defeats the very *idea* of capitalism and rewards failure. If a company is about to go out of business, it is probably because the company did something wrong like— oh, let's see—make subpar products, for example. If GM and Chrysler had spent half the money on car quality over a few decades that they were spending on perks for their union members, they probably would've never needed to take money from taxpayers. Instead, they drove themselves (see what we did there?) into the ground with mostly craptacular cars.

You know what bailout money does? It defeats the very *idea* of capitalism and rewards failure.

In the past, if you didn't like GM or Chrysler, you just didn't buy their stuff. But in 2008? If you didn't like their stuff, that was just too bad—because your tax dollars still went to help get them out of the mess they'd gotten themselves into, whether you liked it or not.

Failure was rewarded. Success was punished. And politicians on both sides of the aisle were responsible. Does that sound like the America our Founding Fathers envisioned? Let us answer that for you. *No*, it does not. And conservatives who balk at the idea of bailouts are right.

POVERTY REDEFINED

Conservatives who argue against corporate bailouts also oppose individual bailouts, which is what many entitlement programs have become. And let's be clear here. Conservatives aren't the heartless, uncompassionate dirtbags that liberals claim we are. We fully support programs that help people who face unfortunate circumstances get back on their feet. We fully support programs that help the sick and disabled and weakest among us. But there's a difference between the weakest among us and what is now known as "the poor."

Most Americans who are officially classified as "poor" in this country live pretty damn well. According to Robert Rector of the *National Review*, the government's data shows that the average "poor" person "has two color televisions, cable or satellite service, a VCR or DVD player, and a stereo. He also has a car, air conditioning, a refrigerator, a stove, a clothes washer and dryer, and a microwave. He is able to obtain medical care. His home is in good repair and is not overcrowded. By his own report, his family is not hungry, and he had sufficient funds in the past year to meet his family's essential needs."[4] Doesn't your heart just bleed for those impoverished folks?

A couple of years ago, Obama announced that he'd be implementing a new poverty-measurement system. His nifty new system tied in really nicely with his goal of taking people's money and distributing it to other people. You know, spreading the wealth around, as he is so often inclined to do.

Here's how the new measurement works. First, if a family's income falls below a certain income threshold, they're considered poor. Second, those thresholds are tied to the living standards of average Americans, rising along with those standards. That's kind of a big deal. Instead of gauging how much a family can *actually buy*, the new measure gauges how much they can buy *compared to others*.

Liberals love this idea. If the country prospers, the definition of "poor" keeps prospering right along with it. So people who receive benefits meant for "the poor" could actually be quite comfortable. That's super handy for people like Obama and other Democrats who count on people counting on *them*. Under Obama's measurement system, the definition of "poor" can only be reduced if the incomes of the poor rise faster than everyone else's.

. . . .

Obama's measuring scale is designed to increase, artificially, the number of Americans classified as poor.

. . . .

As Robert Rector pointed out in his *National Review* article on this subject, poverty rates in countries like Bangladesh and Albania would be lower than ours under this new system of measurement. Never mind that if you're poor in Albania you're probably living outside in a box, while in the United States you're more than likely inside with air-conditioning, watching a flat screen and texting someone on your iPhone.

Obama's measuring scale is designed to increase, artificially, the number of Americans classified as poor. And so all of those poor, wretched people with their two TVs and their air-conditioning could potentially qualify for more of everyone else's money to supplement their horrible living conditions. See how that works? It's how new Democrats are born every day.

In case you're wondering what happened to Obama's nifty new poverty-measurement system, the Census Bureau asserted that an additional three million people fell into the "poor" category immediately after its implementation.[5] And of course by "people" we mean "Democratic voters." Color us unsurprised.

And liberals wonder why conservatives get so sick and tired of having our wealth confiscated "for the common good." *Hello. This is why.*

So the government continues to do what it does best—pour taxpayer money into entitlements without stopping to think for a second that maybe, just maybe, the reasons real poverty is on the rise are high unemployment, a horrendous economic climate for businesses, and the "rewarding" of low-income families for giving birth to multiple kids out of wedlock while at the same time penalizing marriage.

Be proud, conservatives. We are right about capitalism. We're right about championing equal opportunity over equality. We're right about the hope and promise of the American dream, realized by those who work to earn it, not by progressives who expect it'll be handed to them via legislation and wealth redistribution.

THE HARRISON BERGERONIFICATION OF AMERICA

Kurt Vonnegut's short story "Harrison Bergeron" portrays a futuristic America that's the opposite of the American dream. In the story, the Constitution has been amended to declare all Americans equal in every way. No one can be smarter, dumber, stronger, weaker, faster, or slower than anyone else, and a "Handicapper General" with a team of agents makes sure all equality laws are enforced. As you can imagine, life in that America isn't so great.

The story is an eerie picture of what could, and will, happen, if liberalism has its way. You see, the Harrison Bergeronification of America is all about making sure the world is fair, and liberals think fairness is more important than anything else. Unfortunately, if we follow the pursuit of fairness to its inevitable conclusion, everything would actually really suck. Liberals constantly whine about multiculturalism, tolerance, and acceptance, but they don't seem to realize that by pushing for total equality they are advocating for the total demise of individuality. Or maybe they just don't care, because if everyone is equally miserable, well, by golly, at least that's fair.

Liberals constantly whine about multiculturalism, tolerance, and acceptance, but they don't seem to realize that by pushing for total equality they are advocating for the total demise of individuality.

Let's look at the Harrison Bergeronification already happening in America. A couple of years ago, a Chicago school considered dropping its honors English class because there were not enough minority students in it. The school in question prided itself on "embracing diversity and promoting equity and excellence" for all of its students. At the time, freshmen who outscored 95 percent of their peers on a national level were allowed into an elite honors class. The problem was that very few minority students made it in. The school's proposed solution? To get rid of the class altogether, of course.[6] Because we can't have white kids excelling all over the place, now, can we? That wouldn't be fair to all the nonwhite kids who *aren't* excelling.

And it gets better. The copresident of the student council actually said, out loud, "It's time for all students to experience excellence." In other words, it's not fair if only some students make it into the high-level class, since they would be the only ones "experiencing excellence."

Paging Harrison Bergeron . . .

This should go without saying, but if *all* students "experience excellence," then what was once excellent instantly becomes average. Conservatives intuitively understand this. It's why conservative parents don't give out trophies for seventh-place finishes.

Everyone can't be excellent. It's not possible, unless you completely dilute the meaning of excellence. Liberals cannot

MORE WACK FROM THE OWS
ECONOMIC CHARTER

Remember earlier when we told you about the crazy Occupy Wall Street folks' economic charter? The section on education is mind-blowingly Harrison Bergeronified. Check out these choice quotes.

Education should be funded with some of the $2 billion/week that goes to war-funding. At least 50% of it. This will weaken our millitary [sic] by 50% at least, forcing the rest of the world to pick up the slack. This will in turn cause their economies to tank, taking ours with it. But at least we'll be highly educated.

They said this for real, y'all. They *actually suggested* that we should tank our economy, knowingly, willfully, because hey—at least we'll be highly educated, right? *This is how those crazy hippies think.* "We'll be impoverished, jobless, hungry, and miserable, but *by golly, we will be educated.*"

But wait. It gets better. They suggested, "Socialize undergraduate level college. Make failing impossible to assure that everyone has the same chance in the work place post-college."

If you dare to be smarter than the average Joe, like, say, Harrison Bergeron, then they'll just figure out a way to suppress your intellect. No more of this silly competition and working hard nonsense. Everyone should get an A! Failing is impossible, and everyone is excellent. Seems legit.

And of course, all of that excellence should be free:

Free education for all. Use former war expenses and equitable taxation of the rich to develop free public schools, free text books, free higher education. Assure that every student educated in the United States has a guaranteed job or can perform service in some way that recompenses their education. Forgive all current student loans.

In other words, to quote the well-known intellectual powerhouse Britney Spears, "Gimme gimme more."

Now here's the one that should make the hairs on everyone's arms stand up:

Teach character building classes from grade one, measure success based on drive/cooperation/interactions with others, not only final outcome. Impose universal morality for parents who do not participate in raising their children. Remove children from households with parents who refuse to educate them properly. Provide for re-education of parents in how to properly raise their children for the happiness of the party.

Um, say *what*? Universal morality?! So, if you don't raise your kids according to the way these "progressives" see fit, they'll take your kids from you and send you to reeducation camps. Perfect. That should go over well in a free republic.

And check this out. The Occupiers also wanted to ensure the government was addressing the needs of its taxpaying citizens, so their economic charter suggests that the government should be "held accountable for achieving specific Gross National Happiness index target values."

wrap their minds around this. If given the opportunity, they'd rename "average" so that it's called "excellent," tax it somehow, mandate it, and then triumphantly proclaim, *"Look at all the diversity!"* That is how twisted their logic is. "Let's celebrate diversity by mandating that everyone is exactly the same! *Yay!"*

Fairness at all costs. Spread the wealth. Eliminate capitalism. Redistribute. Dumb down the requirements. It's all Harrison Bergeronification. And it's happening.

Which is probably why we're starting to see socialists winning elections.

SOCIALISTS ARE WINNING ELECTIONS, AND THAT SHOULD TERRIFY US

In November 2013, New York City elected a socialist mayor named Bill de Blasio. Seattle voters also went to the polls and willingly elected a socialist named Kshama Sawant to their city council. Mind you, neither of these two candidates ran under the guise of anything other than blatant "spread the wealth" socialism and opposition to capitalism. And yet, Americans living in a free republic went straight to their polling booths and voted for these jackwagons.

Something about these candidates spoke to the lobotomized lemmings, you see. The message of "Here's your free crap, comrades!" resonated the loudest with them. Frightening, isn't it?

That is where we are today in America. We are at a point where the takers have officially outweighed the makers, and the new narrative of "what's theirs is mine" and "you owe me something" is so firmly planted in the skulls of the masses now, it's normal. It's *trendy*, even. Like Uggs.

Which are heinous, too, by the way. So stop with those already.

These days MSNBC has been preaching the merits of "mincome," a certain level of annual income guaranteed to everyone by the government. Canadian liberals experimented with it back in the 1970s, and though the project lasted only five years, the Left loves to yap about how awesome it was.[7] All families received a "minimum cash benefit," which helped them spend more time with one another, helped kids graduate from high school, and even cut down on hospital visits, as there were fewer on-the-job injuries (because—you guessed it—people weren't freaking working. . . . *hello*). The thing that liberals forget about this type of experiment is that money doesn't magically appear out of thin air or get manufactured from unicorn farts and puppy kisses. While the Canadian mincome project may have been a success for its five-year run, it wasn't—and never could be—sustainable. Projects like this will always, inevitably, run out of other people's money. But the biggest lesson learned from this experiment is that reality doesn't make for good messaging.

Reality isn't *sexy*, y'all.

What *does* make for good messaging? Well, offer a hungry kid a choice between broccoli or cake with sprinkles for dinner, and what will that kid choose? Substitute the kid for a liberal, the cake with sprinkles for a Democrat, and the broccoli for a Republican, and you have the messaging scenario of the last two elections. That's why socialists are now winning elections in America. Democrats are, without question, the cake-and-sprinkles party these days. They have won a bedazzled–popularity contest by promising free stuff and spinning their message to sound hip. Republicans are the broccoli party—what we offer is really good for everyone, but our message is not sexy. You're never going to see financial pragmatism or personal responsibility get its own reality show on E!, people.

· ·

Republicans are the broccoli party—what we offer is really good for everyone, but our message is not sexy.

· ·

By Democrat design and our default, we've become the social-issues party instead of sticking to the strength of our fiscal message. And we completely *suck* at social issues. We're seen as that boring, lackluster party that somehow dislikes gays, women, and poor people, so, naturally, we lose elections. And this is maddening to those of us that know the truth about the conservative message. Those of us who are shouting to anyone who will listen, "We are the party of personal fiscal responsibility, capitalism, smaller government, and *don't freaking tread on me!*"

All people see is the broccoli. And, ew, broccoli. No one wants *that.*

Gimme some cake.

ACTUALLY, MR. PRESIDENT, WE DID BUILD THIS

On July 13, 2012, President Obama said something out loud that became the defining phrase of his campaign:

> *If you were successful, somebody along the line gave you some help. There was a great teacher somewhere in your life. Somebody helped to create this unbelievable American system that we have that allowed you to thrive. Somebody invested in roads and bridges. If you've got a business—you didn't build that. Somebody else made that happen.*[8]

Oh, no, he didn't.

More than likely, you remember the backlash. The Romney campaign, of course, jumped all over it, and the Internet memes were rampant. Phrases like this tend to piss you off when you're working two jobs, and you actually *have* built something out of nothing with no help from the almighty government. You know.

When we first started our humble little Chicks on the Right blog back in February 2009, we did it with absolutely no money, and little to no web experience. What we did have, though, was a drive to work hard, an optimistic outlook, and the belief that we had nothing to lose and everything to gain.

This is America, after all. And besides, it's like they say in the movie *Field of Dreams*. If you build it, people will come, right?

In the beginning, we got excited when we saw five simultaneous readers on the site—even if a handful of them happened to be our parents. But we always had hope that our little venture would eventually take off and thrive. The sky was the limit, and we were bright-eyed and filled with high expectations, even though we had absolutely no idea what we were doing. But we were raised to believe that if we worked hard, and if we put in our blood, sweat, tears, and passion, we'd eventually see the fruits of our labor pay off. That's what good ol' American capitalism is all about.

So that's what we did. We worked our assular areas off, in fact. There were a lot of late nights and early mornings spent on growing and building our happy little corner of the Internet. At the same time, we had to figure out ways to perform well in our full-time careers, spend time with our families, maintain relationships with friends, and not completely lose our minds in the process. We sacrificed and interrupted family time and cut short way too many social ventures. Sleep became a special treat instead of just a nighttime ritual.

The work was hard, but it paid off. Little by little, we started seeing improvements in our bottom line. The couple hundred bucks we made in advertising was invested right back into the site. Traffic started to grow, and we hired a webmaster who actually knew what in the heck he was doing to make the design of the site more appealing and more functional. We made countless mistakes along the way, but we never gave up on the one thing we were fully invested in—the American dream.

And here we are. Five years later, we still work just as hard, but we're starting to finally reap some benefits from the hard work we've put in, and we're also seeing the rewards of having built a community. Real friendships have developed, and many of our "regulars" travel across the country to see each other. Hundreds of thousands of people follow our site now (in addition to our parents!), though we're just two nobodies from the heartland without a lick of experience in building a website—let alone a whole brand.

But here we are.

We've built a political community of like-minded folks through sheer determination and a hell of a lot of sweat equity. And we've made it our life's work.

You hear that, Mr. President? *We built that.* We can appreciate the point the president was trying to make—that success comes not from the initiative of a single individual but the culmination of the efforts of many. For example, we Chicks would certainly credit our parents with raising us right. We'd credit our husbands with giving us the space and time we needed to be able to devote our energy to our website. We'd credit high school teachers who taught us how to type, perhaps. We'd even credit Obama himself for saying enough stupid crap to provide fodder for our website for years to come. But *come on*. That's not what Obama was talking about. It's when he's unscripted and un-teleprompted that his true colors are revealed. In that moment, he was totally transparent. He genuinely believes that private-sector businesses owe their success to government. Because *infrastructure*, you guys. And roads and bridges and public education and stuff. Never mind that it's taxpayers who *pay* for the infrastructure, and never mind that those taxpayers include the business owners themselves. Obama views government as the foundation of any successful enterprise. Period.

Worse still is that in many people's view, government isn't just the foundation; it's the salvation as well. And that is wack.

Conservatives are right to revere the notion of a free-market, capitalist system. It's the economic foundation upon which this country was built. Money is a good thing, and so is the equal opportunity to earn it. Liberals who don't buy that (pun intended) and who feel justified in robbing the wealthy of what they've rightfully earned while they're screaming about equality and fairness are shining beacons of hypocrisy, because they are the ones being completely unfair.

CHAPTER 2

America Is Exceptional

We're unabashedly, shamelessly devoted to the idea of our country's exceptionalism. In other words, we believe that this great country of ours is certainly different from and generally better than other nations. It's not that Americans are inherently better than other people; it's that the ideas upon which our country was founded are truly exceptional. And that's why we are so fortunate to live here. That's also why so many others who weren't born in the United States are chomping at the bit to cross the border and experience the greatness for themselves. It's a popular place, the United States of America. Because it's freaking exceptional.

It's right for conservatives to be proud and patriotic and filled with reverence and love for our country. America is the land of opportunity, founded on the inalienable rights of life, liberty, and the pursuit of happiness. The United States has a unique role in the world—to advance the cause of freedom and shine as a beacon of liberty to every other nation. America, to the extent that it sticks to those values, is the example to be followed—the gold standard against which other nations should try to measure themselves.

Which is why we don't take kindly to people like Obama

trying to "fundamentally transform" our country into something it was never supposed to be.

Think about it. Is there anything more demoralizing than a president who downplays our exceptionalism, and worse still, *apologizes* to other countries on our behalf? That's precisely what Obama has done. Oh, sure, the Obama campaign insists that conservatives are wrong about Obama's "apology tour"— that in fact, Obama never apologized for America at all—but let's be real here. Obama clearly isn't all that enthralled with America or the foundation upon which it was built, because if he were, he wouldn't be so hell-bent on trying to transform it.

As we've said, America freaking rocks. But here's the thing. We conservatives can cheerlead and wave our flags all we want, but our nation's exceptionalism is at risk. It pains us to say it, but it's true. Liberals, who already are quick to badmouth our country, are perpetuating victimhood, stifling entrepreneurship, encouraging dependency, and promoting collectivism. If this trend continues, Americans will not only catch the liberal bad attitude toward America, but they'll be justified in thinking it's not so great. Because if liberalism takes over, it won't be.

AMERICAN EXCEPTIONALISM JUST ISN'T COOL ANYMORE

Back in September 2013, Pew Research conducted a survey and asked people if they thought that the United States was indeed the greatest country in the world. Of those questioned, 48 percent said that yes, we were exceptional. But there was a generational divide, with most adults 65 and older saying the United States was the world's greatest country, but only half of those 35–64 and a third of those 18–34 agreed with that statement. Not surprisingly, there was also a partisan divide, with a larger percentage of Republicans than Democrats agreeing that America is the greatest nation on earth.[1]

The political landscape has changed in this country, and the once-ingrained idea of American exceptionalism is now considered fringe thought. And the younger the demographic, the more American exceptionalism fades. This can be partly attributed to the liberal stranglehold on the media, but it's also because we are witnessing senators like Harry Reid demonizing—on the Senate floor (and on the taxpayer dime, no less)—private citizens such as the Koch brothers for being *successful entrepreneurs.* We're witnessing talk-show hosts like Bill Maher losing their minds because of Cadillac advertisements that exemplify free-market capitalism and American exceptionalism, joking about how hardworking we are at the expense of other countries.[2] Because it's *smug* to talk about having nice cars, you greedy, filthy Americans! As a result of all the negativity, we're witnessing our young people becoming politically complacent—they just don't have the same kind of pride in their country that the generations before them did.

While being told that the American ideals of hard work are stupid, these kids have also been taught that the government is there to *give them stuff* from cradle to grave. Democrats have taught this generation that they can get money for nothing and their health insurance for free. So how on God's green earth can kids respect a country that is nothing more to them than a faceless ATM machine?

The bottom line is that we are not going to be exceptional if we don't get off our butts and take action. And that means intercepting and changing the anti-American narratives becoming more prevalent in our schools.

EDUCATION'S ATTACK ON AMERICAN EXCEPTIONALISM

American civics education has become weak and apologetic. When we were growing up, we were taught that in order to make anything out of ourselves, we had to work hard. And we weren't just taught that at home. We were taught that through the public school system. Back in the day, public schools weren't overrun by administrators with degrees in diversity and multiculturalism. Our teachers taught us that America was the greatest nation on earth. We sang the entire songbook of John Philip Sousa songs in our choir classes. We said the Pledge of Allegiance with reverence every morning. If we misbehaved, there was a wooden paddle hanging ominously over the teacher's desk and the threat of a trip to the principal's office, where we knew it'd be used on our butts if the offense was grave enough.

Things are different now. You hear stories every day about radically progressive educators attempting to impose anti-American curricula on students. These education officials want more diversity studies, more "institutional racism" studies, and more teaching on the evils of capitalism. You hear about people filing lawsuits so that kids aren't forced to participate in the unthinkable practice of standing and reciting the Pledge of Allegiance. This is the world we live in now.

You have to wonder why progressives are so hell-bent on wanting America's children to grow up hating their own country so much. If American citizens treat our country like this, it's no wonder that foreign leaders feel free to criticize us.

CALDERÓN AND OBAMA SITTIN' IN A TREE

Back in the summer of 2010, then-president of Mexico Felipe Calderón was invited to speak to Congress on the House floor. His speech came right in the midst of the controversy surrounding Arizona's SB 1070—legislation that effectively allowed law enforcement in Arizona to actually protect the state's own border. Let us just refresh your memory on a few of the things Calderón said in a speech he made to the members of the U.S. Congress:

> *I am convinced that comprehensive immigration reform is also crucial to secure our common border. However, I strongly disagree with the recently adopted law in Arizona. It is a law that not only ignores a reality that cannot be erased by decree but also introduces a terrible idea: using racial profiling as a basis for law enforcement. And that is why I agree with President Obama, who said the new law "carries a great amount of risk when core values that we all care about are breached."*[3]

Calderón had the audacity to essentially condemn one of our nation's fifty states in the middle of the floor of the U.S. Capitol building in front of our elected representatives. That actually happened. For real.

During the same visit, Presidents Obama and Calderón also took to the White House lawn to jointly attack Arizona for having the gall to try to enforce border laws that mirror federal laws already on the books. They were basically falling all over each other to see who would win the I Hate the Arizona Law Most contest. Calderón said the law "forced his people to face discrimination" and he called for a "border that would unite us instead of dividing us." (Translation: If you could just go ahead and make it easier for our people to walk over the border illegally without penalty or consequence, that'd be terrific. In fact, if you could also provide refreshments along the way, we'd appreciate it.)

Calderón also said, "We will retain our firm rejection to criminalized migration so that people that work and provide things to this nation would be treated as criminals." Hey,

Calderón, crossing the border illegally is a crime—hence the whole, you know, *criminality* of it. OMG.

· ·

Obama declared, "We're not defined by our borders." What the hell? If you look at a world map, that's precisely what we're defined by.

· ·

And Obama was no better. Obama declared, "We're not defined by our borders." What the hell? If you look at a world map, that's precisely what we're defined by. That's why a world map isn't just a bunch of landmasses without names on them.

Liberals cheered this entire display. Democrats jumped to their feet to give Calderón a standing ovation on the House floor. They applauded Calderón sticking his nose right into our domestic affairs, and ripping on our policies, right in the middle of the floor of the people's house.

Conservatives everywhere were outraged by this, and with good reason. Because it's one thing to criticize your own family, but when outsiders criticize your family, you bristle. And for crying out loud, you definitely don't *cheer them on*.

Enter Rep. Tom McClintock, who expressed beautifully what patriotic conservatives were feeling. Shortly after Calderón's speech on the House floor, Representative McClintock gave one of his own for the record, and it really spoke to our conservative, America-loving hearts. He said, in part:

> *I rise to take strong exception to the speech of the president of Mexico while in this chamber today.*
> *The Mexican government has made it very clear for many years that it holds American sovereignty*

in contempt, and President Calderón's behavior as a guest of the Congress confirms and underscores this attitude.

It is highly inappropriate for the president of Mexico to lecture Americans on American immigration policy, just as it would be for Americans to lecture Mexico on its laws.[4]

Boom. Thank God *someone* in Congress had the balls to recognize how inappropriate Calderón was. He went on:

Unlike Mexico's immigration law—which is brutally exclusionary—the purpose of America's law is not to keep people out. It is to assure that as people come to the United States, they do so with the intention of becoming Americans and of raising their children as Americans.

Unlike Mexico, our nation embraces immigration, and what makes that possible is assimilation.

That is how we have built one great nation from the people of all the nations of the world.

That is the broader meaning of our nation's motto, "E pluribus unum"—from many people, one people, the American people.

In other words, we're a melting pot and always have been, which is why people coming to the United States should freaking melt already. Liberals seem to want to destroy what makes this country great, and undermining the assimilation—the melting into the pot—is part of that destruction.

Finally, McClintock went on to really tear Calderón—and the moronic Democrats who supported him—a new one:

*It is an outrage that a foreign head of state would appear in
this chamber and actively seek to do so [undermine our immigration laws]. And it is a disgrace that he would be
cheered on from the left wing of the White House and by
many Democrats in this Congress.*

And *that* was the line that really made us want to grab Representative McClintock and plant like twelve zillion kisses on
his face.

See, that's the difference between liberals and conservatives. Liberals stand up and applaud a foreign leader who rips
on their country on their own soil. Conservatives don't take
that crap lying down. We get all up in that foreign leader's grill.

This is *America*.

"CHANGE THAT BELIEVES IN YOU"

Conservatives think differently about our nation than our liberal counterparts. Liberals are constantly trying to place political authority in the hands of our elected representatives,
convinced that government is the answer to every problem.
Conservatives want just the opposite. We understand that we
the people are in charge, because that's what our founders intended. That's the way our country was designed. That's why
we are exceptional.

Rep. Paul Ryan once said that Americans "want to choose
the path of American exceptionalism, not managed decline."
Our beloved former governor Mitch Daniels transformed
Obama's 2008 campaign slogan "Change You Can Believe In"
into a more substantive one, "Change That Believes in You,"
because he had unwavering faith in the American people to
do the right thing. He was convinced that Americans would
collectively opt to be free and responsible for their own lives

rather than submit to dictatorial leadership telling them that government knows best.

We have to hope that Mitch is right. And that Paul Ryan is right. And we have to do everything we can to help our fellow citizens walk the path of American exceptionalism, too, by reminding them of the ideas that have made us great.

MIRIAM'S FIRST-GENERATION-AMERICAN TALE

It's common for children of immigrants to become exceptionally proud Americans, as a Pew Research Center report indicated in early 2013.[5] I'm a walking example of that, as a first-generation American born to Polish immigrants. My parents, whom my sister and I affectionately call "the Birds" because of their tiny stature, fled and escaped an oppressive, anti-Semitic government. They risked never seeing their families again and came to America to pursue the American dream against incredible odds.

For Christmas 2012, the Birds gave my sister and me a bound first-person account of their life story, written with painstaking, loving detail by my sweet Birdmom. It told the tale of her childhood growing up on a farm without electricity or plumbing. It described my dad's escape with his mother to the Soviet Union when Germany invaded Poland in 1939. His grandmother, after whom I'm named, stayed behind and ultimately died in the Treblinka death camp northeast of Warsaw.

My parents described in great detail their loss of citizenship from their home country, their days in Italy (where I was conceived) while they belonged to no country at all, their early work in science (and my dad's serendipitous hiring by a neurobiologist who ultimately won a Nobel Peace Prize), and their incredible journey to the United States, where they settled in

Ithaca, New York, so my dad could get his PhD at Cornell. My mom worked in the USDA Plant, Soil, and Nutrition lab in which another Nobel Prize winner had determined the sequence of the first nucleic acid the year prior.

The Birds' story, which I read through puddles and puddles of tears, included the description of the day they became American citizens in August of 1974, when I was five years old. They were required to prove that they understood English by writing "I live in America," a hilarious test since my dad had just gotten a PhD at Cornell. They had to pass a citizenship exam, and they had to get letters of reference, one of which was from one of my mom's former bosses, a man named James Madison.

My parents recounted details about their life together that my sister and I had never heard, as well as lots of stories that we remember living personally. They described the visits that I made to Poland with my mother when I was six and when I was ten, but also listed the many times that my mom's requests for a Polish visa were denied, forcing her to spend years without ever seeing her parents or family. They told the story of my father's parents' involvement in the Solidarity movement in Poland before it ultimately succeeded, and my mom recorded memories of visits she made to Poland in the 1980s, during which she personally witnessed the empty food stores and the lines for bread. To help her family when she wasn't visiting, she sent them twenty-dollar bills hidden in seed packages or peanut butter jars, hoping the authorities would not find and confiscate them.

When my mom returned to the States after each visit to Poland, there was nothing like hearing the folks in customs at the airport say, "Welcome home." She still gets choked up every time. Because she and my father are *Americans*, you see. And this is home.

There is an epilogue included in their story specifically devoted to their reflections about America. And in the spirit of the discussion of American exceptionalism, it's worth sharing part of it here, because there are never too many reminders of how lucky we all are to live in this amazing country. She wrote:

> *My appreciation for this country grew over the years, especially after my visits to communist Poland. Every time I went there I had the impression that I was seeing a depressing black and white movie, and as soon as I landed back in the USA, the movie was joyful and in color. Still, for quite a long time I was envious of the Western European welfare system. . . . why could we not have it in America? I just did not understand then all the pitfalls of the welfare state.*
>
> *I realized that America has a unique role in the world, defending freedom, democracy, human rights, and all the right causes around the world, and that it was an expensive endeavor, especially during the Cold War. It required a strong defense, and the people of America took the financial burden of keeping the rest of the world at peace on their own shoulders. The true riches of a country are not measured by the size of its mansions or number of cars, but by its history, its institutions, and character. When we look at those, America stands above and apart from other nations as a truly exceptional country.*

It's worth fighting for, our America.

CHAPTER 3

Hand Ups, Not Handouts

Back in 2013, a Texas convenience-store clerk was taking a customer's Lone Star Card (Texas's card version of food stamps), when he realized that the presumably needy customer's card balance exceeded $7,000. That's a hell of a lot of Big Gulps, huh? And it's a great deal more than what most of us lowly taxpayers make in several months at our full-time jobs.

This wasn't the first time the clerk had noticed large balances. In fact, he had seen people with similar card balances walk into his store time and time again. Fed up with what he considered to be genuine fraud of the system, he reported the incident to his local authorities only to be told by those in charge that there was nothing he could do about it.

It wasn't until a local news affiliate actually covered the story that local politicians miraculously started to pay attention.[1] After expressing their shock and dismay that this type of fraud happens in our perfect, utopian society (we rolled our eyes, too), they promised the great taxpayers of Texas that they would pass legislation that would cap the balance of welfare-recipient accounts, and they promised the accounts would be regularly audited. Because promises of legislation solve everything. And we're sure Texas taxpayers felt *much* better knowing some guy in a suit somewhere was working on it.

On a side note, in that one Texas county alone, there are more than 238,000 people on SNAP, which costs taxpayers more than $28 million per *month*. So, we can see why that clerk was a little peeved when he kept seeing all of those "down and out" folks driving up to his convenience store in their mack-daddy Mercedes, with surplus amounts on their taxpayer-funded credit cards, while the rest of us were toiling away at our jobs. You know, funding their lifestyles while trying to make ends meet for our families.

There's a problem in this country with entitlement. It's out of control. It's an ugly, crippling disease that is eating away at the great work ethic America has always been known for. The takers are well on their way to officially outnumbering the makers, and honestly, who can blame people for their dependency on government when liberals spend so much time creating policies and programs that encourage that very dependency?

There is a time and a place for welfare. We believe in safety nets. We believe in helping people. We believe that the weakest among us and the people who are down on their luck should get assistance. But a safety net is just that—a net. It's a temporary holding place, not a place to live forever. Our government is pouring so much money into entitlements that this net has turned into a hammock. In fact, a Cato Institute report from 2013 concluded that welfare pays more than minimum-wage work in thirty-five states, making it to people's benefit to live off entitlements instead of working. People have forgotten that they should work to earn their livings, and instead they simply accept the handouts.

· ·

There is a time and a place for welfare. We believe in safety nets. We believe in helping people. We believe that the weakest among us and the people who are down on their luck should get assistance. But a safety net is just that—a net.

· ·

Meanwhile, policy-making liberals don't care that they're bankrupting the country because they are too ignorant to realize that money for entitlement programs doesn't simply materialize out of thin air. They're convinced that if those mean, greedy rich people would just "pay their fair share," then everyone would live happily ever after. How many times was the phrase "fair share" drilled into the American psyche during the last two election cycles? Liberals love to paint conservatives as big ol' selfish meanies, and they'll keep right on doing that right until they run out of those big ol' selfish meanies' money. And that won't help anyone.

The reality, though, is that conservatives are demonstrably more compassionate and charitable than we're ever given credit for, and we are right to believe that it takes *actual effort* to achieve the American dream. It's right that we are reluctant to provide "something for nothing" to parasitic leeches. We conservatives are right to expect that able-bodied people have skin in the game when it comes to lifting themselves out of poverty. And we're typically the first in line to offer a hand up to folks who genuinely need help.

In fact, as Arthur Brooks's book *Who Really Cares: The Surprising Truth About Compassionate Conservatism* points out, people who oppose the redistribution of wealth as a way to combat income inequality (i.e., conservatives) give over *ten times* more to charity than those who strongly support government programs (i.e., liberals).[2] Conservative heads of household, it turns out, additionally give 30 percent more money to charity than their liberal counterparts, even though for the year studied, liberal-headed households earned 6 percent more per year.

And even Nicholas Kristof, a giant in liberal circles, wrote an op-ed in the *New York Times* shamelessly berating fellow liberals to give more, citing Brooks's book but also other independent studies proving the same thing—that conservatives are far more giving to those in need than liberals. "Come on liberals," he pleaded, "redeem yourselves, and put your wallets where your hearts are."[3]

We don't need government to force us to be charitable. We need government to get the hell out of our way so we can more freely help those in need. For all of the "help" that government has sought to provide the needy, they sure haven't moved the needle much.

PROSPERITY IN THE UNITED STATES IS ON THE DECLINE NO MATTER HOW MUCH MONEY IS THROWN INTO ENTITLEMENTS

The government's answer to everything is to throw money at it, despite mounds and mounds of evidence that doing so doesn't work. Unfortunately, the money being poured into entitlements has been successful at one thing—creating a shift in Americans' attitudes about work and rewards. According to the Legatum Institute's annual Prosperity Index, even though prosperity *increased* around the world between 2008 and 2012, it didn't budge in the United States. In 2012, for the first time ever, the United States ranked outside the top ten out of 142 countries, at number twelve on the Prosperity Index.[4]

The reasons? The ones conservatives have been shrieking about for the past several years—a decline in entrepreneurship and economic opportunity. *Hello.*

The authors of the index said that the United States' fall in prosperity was "driven by a decline in the number of US citizens who believe that hard work will get them ahead." Further, "the typical American's attitude has shifted, ever so subtly, away from a belief that free markets and entrepreneurship are central to economic prosperity."

In other words, people actually bought into the Occupy Wall Street message of "Capitalism Sucks."

Sigh.

Around the same time that index was released, Nicholas Kristof (again, a hero to many liberals), wrote a column that addressed the dependency on government programs.[5] He focused on Kentucky's Appalachian area, where people have yanked their kids out of literacy classes because if those kids learn to read, the parents will be less likely to qualify for a monthly SSI check for having kids with intellectual disabilities. We are not even making this up.

Apparently, many of these people receive nearly $700 each month from Supplemental Security Income for those "disabled" children, and they receive those payments until their kids turn eighteen. And when the kids *do* turn eighteen, they are illiterate and unproductive because of their parents, and they collect SSI income as adults, many of them never holding a job in their entire lives. This is how our entitlement programs "help." Nice, huh?

Kristof wrote, "This is painful for a liberal to admit, but conservatives have a point when they suggest that America's safety net can sometimes entangle people in a soul-crushing dependency. Our poverty programs do rescue many people, but other times they backfire."

Another example of the backfiring: many young people now find it's far easier to rely on food stamps and disability checks than it is to enlist in the armed forces. And the *government has made it that way.*

Worse, SSI income is bigger if a woman raises kids alone instead of *marrying the father,* another example of a marriage penalty embedded within an entitlement program. As Kristof argues, "Marriage is one of the best forces to blunt poverty. In married couple households only one child in 10 grows up in poverty, while almost half do in single mother households." So naturally, our government does the best it can to discourage marriage. Brilliant!

· ·

Many young people now find it's far easier to rely on food stamps and disability checks than it is to enlist in the armed forces. And the *government has made it that way.*

· ·

As depressing as that all is, Kristof's column gave us hope that even liberals recognize the problem. *Finally.* As Kristof admits in the most astute line from his column, "The bottom line is that we shouldn't try to fight poverty with a program that sometimes perpetuates it."

Which brings us back to the Prosperity Index. You can't tell us that our falling prosperity is not linked to a growing belief that hard work just isn't worth the potential payoff.

Not to sound callous, but if people are not incentivized to put in some effort to be productive, we fail to see how continuing to simply hand them everything they need is helpful to anyone, including them. All we're doing is creating generations of unproductive, dependent parasites.

As Kristof's column makes clear, liberals can't deny that research shows the most effective strategies to combat these issues are to work early on children and education, and to encourage and sustain marriage. Furthermore, you can't deny that when it comes to poverty, liberals shoulder a lot of blame. They are to blame for making stupid laws that drive businesses and jobs overseas. They are to blame for creating the culture of entitlement and dependency. They are to blame for creating policies that have driven our country into more debt than is even imaginable, in record time to boot.

We're right about this. We're right about the idea of offering a hand up to people in need, and not just providing a handout. We're right about how entitlement programs enslave more than they empower. Fortunately, as many ordinary Americans know, there's a better way.

LESLIE'S STORY

In the summer of 2013, we received a heartbreaking letter from a woman named Leslie, who wrote:

> *Dear Chicks:*
>
> *This is something that I felt compelled to write.*
>
> *I am very conservative. I am a Christian who is very staunch on my beliefs. But . . . I am also a member of the "working poor" of this country.*
>
> *I work 32 hours a week, grooming dogs, for $8.00 an hour. I go to college part time, seated and online. I am a single mother of a precocious 5 year old girl. And, right*

now, we are homeless. I cannot afford any healthcare for myself as bringing home approx. $210.00 a week, I make too much for Medicaid, but not nearly enough to afford to buy it. Thankfully, in NC, my daughter does have Medicaid.

We also get around $200.00 a month in EBT (or food stamps). I also get a partial daycare subsidy, as $150.00 a week for daycare is way out of my price range. Yes, I am on the system. But, I am also 47 years old, and have paid into this system for 30 years. It took a long time to accept that I am in the position that these grants were originally created for. Am I proud to be on this system? Hell no. But I do it for my daughter. I do it because there are not enough jobs that pay more than minimum wage. I have no family. It is just my daughter and myself. I have nobody to help me watch her so that I can work nights or weekends. And, to be honest, I don't WANT to work then. This child I have is a miracle, and one that came later in my life. I am already missing too much of her life by dropping her off at daycare at 7:20am and picking her up at 5:30pm. By the time we get back to the house, we have about 30 minutes together before I have to get her ready for bed. I am missing too much of her life as it is, time I will never get back. So, I want to work days. But, decent paying jobs in this town are few and far between. Being a town that centers around the largest military base on the east coast, most working women here are dependents, and they are just supplementing income. Turnover is so high here with families relocating constantly, that employers do not feel they have to raise wages, as there will always be someone to fill the positions.

So, I am working until I am in pain, going to college trying to do better, raising a child alone, and struggling beyond anything I ever thought imaginable. This is our second bout with homelessness. In Dec, 2011, we entered a homeless shelter in another part of the state, as I had lost my good paying job while caring for my terminally ill mother. After Mom passed we had nothing and after a few nights sleeping in the car, we entered the shelter on Dec 20th. We moved to this section of the state NOT because I have a great job, or great home, but because this county was the last county in the state that had no waiting list for daycare subsidy. Where I was, I had lost my voucher when I lost my job. And if I had gotten another job, I would have been on a waiting list 8–12 months long. You can't get a job if you don't have daycare, you can't get daycare if you don't have a job. As it is, 12 days after we moved to this county, they went on a waiting list. That list is now 9 months long and growing.

The place we were renting was horrific and dangerous, but it was a roof, until I could no longer afford it. Now I am in the position of not having enough money to even look for a place . . . but I have to keep my job or I will lose our voucher. I am stuck. We are currently living with a friend from our church, but this will not last, and I am actively looking for another home, but, honestly, I cannot even afford $400 a month as it is half of what I take home. Add in power, my phone (prepaid . . . I did NOT take the "Obamaphone" even though I qualified for it), daycare, car payment, car insurance, gas for the car (which increases daily), tithes and basic essentials, and I am already in the red. All places I have looked at for roommates do not want a young child in their home. So, I am basically stuck.

Obama and his policies have ruined things. There are no incentives to help someone who is working hard and trying *to get ahead. There are no incentives to give any hands up at all. It is all hands out. I was flat out told if I quit my job, I would be "entitled" to more help, including rental, food and Medicaid. But, what am I teaching my daughter by doing this? I will not sit on my ass with my hand out, I am just asking for a hand up. But I have seen FIRST HAND, people who have come into this country, do not even speak the language, come into DSS and walk up to the counter and ask for a translator, and get walked in back. They get Medicaid, they have kids in this country and get all sorts of help from our country, while putting nothing back into the coffers. There are even FREE clinics that provide medical care to the "undocumented" while I, who have paid taxes for 30 years and NEED medical attention, cannot get any care. Remember, that even though I am on the system, I am still paying into it as well. I see people at the DSS who drive MUCH nicer cars than I do, wear MUCH nicer clothes, wear jewelry that I would never dream of owning, and talking on iPhones. While I drive up in my 2003 Neon that still is not paid for, in my Goodwill jeans and $6.00 shoes, and struggle with my sadly out of date phone to find a signal.*

And this fiasco that is Obamacare. . . .

As someone who makes far below the FPL for a family of 2, I would have been one of the ones covered under the Medicaid expansion. But, since NC has now opted out of this plan, I will probably have no insurance and yet still have to pay in my taxes. And, newsflash, even though we were promised our taxes would not go up, my taxes did indeed go up! Now, $8 a week may not sound like much, but that comes to $416.00 a year . . . or, half a month's worth of wages. When you are living penny to penny as it is, that amount DOES make a difference. Now, I would not be *adverse to my taxes rising if there was something positive to show for it, but there is nothing.*

Sometimes when I see my fellow conservatives going on about the system and people who use it, I cringe. I was once one of those people. God drastically changed my circumstances and now I see it from this side. I am not proud of having to be where I am, but I am not seeing any way out at the moment. I wish I could move to an area where there are more opportunities, but it would just be more of the same. I think we need to make things easier to help people get up . . . but the current state of welfare is actually devised to keep people dependent. All the things I have seen from this side, we need to stop paying people to be lazy and help those who are trying to do better. But the liberals want to keep the poor poor, (funny, that's what they say about the conservatives). The poor just cannot see how they are being made to be more and more dependent upon this government. When they finally do see, it may well be too late. It is a game of control, and they are being led to slaughter.

So, here I am . . . lost at sea.

But I am still on the right. I still believe in this country. I still believe we can recapture the glory we had. And maybe the system can be restructured to be what it was intended to be: Something to help people who have fallen to get back up, and not give to those too lazy to get up. Or those who cross the border with their hands immediately out.

We are a small number of conservative poor . . . but we are here.

Thank you for listening,
Leslie

When we shared Leslie's letter with our readers, we wrote that we were amazed by the fact that despite the hardships Leslie had faced and continued to face, she was still determined to show her daughter what it meant to do the right thing. She saw how the system worked firsthand—how it is designed to keep people enslaved, dependent, and bound to their government master. The fact that she hadn't just settled back and accepted the handouts without making an effort to claw her way out of her situation was remarkable, given how much easier that would have been.

While we felt encouraged by Leslie's sense of honor and humility and her incredible work ethic, we felt hopeless about the number of Leslies in our country who suffer at the hands of liberal policies designed to keep them down. Liberals constantly screech about compassion for the poor and needy, accusing conservatives of hating the poor, but it's liberals who continue to demand money for programs that *do not help* the needy. Compassion isn't about government programs. Compassion is about doing the right things for the economy to incentivize employers to create jobs and entrepreneurs to create new businesses, so that the Leslies of the world have opportunities to crawl out of the dependency hole. Compassion isn't telling people to quit a job so they can qualify for more government programs. It's giving people the tools they need to find better employment, and ensuring that the safety nets that are in place aren't a better option than an actual job. Entitlement programs should be a last resort, not a job alternative.

Liberals constantly screech about compassion for the poor and needy, accusing conservatives of hating the poor, but it's liberals who continue to demand money for programs that *do not help* the needy.

Even though we felt hopelessness about Leslie's situation, it didn't last, because we soon discovered the amazing compassion of conservatives. The response to our post about Leslie was overwhelming. Our readers were as horrified at her situation as we were and wanted to know what they could do to help.

We reached out to Leslie to let her know our community was desperate to help her in some way. We also went through the necessary steps to verify both her identity and her situation, and we talked to our accountant to figure out the best way for our online community to help her financially. Ultimately, we decided to raise money to pay off her car so she could travel to work without the looming fear of having her vehicle repossessed. The balance on her car loan was about $4,500, and we set up a fund-raising site for her so that people could send in donations. We posted the link to the donation page at 8:30 a.m. one day, and by 11:00 a.m. that same day, we'd collected $6,000—enough to pay off Leslie's car and give her some extra cash on top. Additionally, dozens of our readers sent Leslie household goods and clothes and toys, and some even sent her offers of jobs and temporary housing. In short, it was an incredible demonstration of how willing conservatives are to help people in need. Particularly those who so desperately want to help themselves, and not just take someone else's money thanklessly.

Leslie's reaction was priceless:

I never, in my wildest dreams, expected the outcome of that letter.

To say I am overwhelmed is an understatement! And grateful. So grateful. I'm keeping my car and I can keep my job. If I had lost the car that was going to be it. Game over. With it I am able to still work, and try and find a better job and continue to look for a home for us.

On the home front, we are working on getting on the list for low income apartments. I have a meeting with the manager of the complex tomorrow to finish the paperwork and pray it all goes through smoothly. If it does, we could possibly have an apartment within 3–5 months!!

I can't wait to tell Kaiya when she gets older about how people out there DO care. That this country does have good people in it, no matter what it looks like to the outsider. She will always know of every kind act, so that she will know how to act towards others when it is our time to give.

And thank you for showing the world the TRUE face of conservatism!!! How can they argue with something this awesome??

Fast-forward to Christmas 2013. Leslie wrote:

The past year has been such a miracle in our lives, and you, and your readers, are a huge part of that. You see, when I wrote that first note, I was pretty much full of despair and frustration. I had no clue how I was going to pay off a car, get us a home, and just have a semi normal life.

The response to the letter did so much for us! It was more than most people realized. First off, it gave me a sliver of hope that this country still had heart. That there was still good, and good people. Not only did we not lose the car, I was able to finish the semester with a pretty solid B average . . . not bad since we were uprooted and unstable during the whole semester. When we finally got into our apartment, we were given gift cards to help us get needed things to start our home. People sent Kaiya clothes and household things. People, complete strangers, helped us and gave us so much.

One amazing thing I was given, was hope. A hope for the future of our country. As long as there are people standing strong, and doing things together to help build up and not knock down, and as long as people have a heart for others, and come together as a group to get something good done, then we have hope. Let the haters say what they want. They should see what kind acts have wrought. It was not a hand out, but a hand UP.

I have not just let it all be in vain. I am working towards doing better. I have been picking up extra work here and there as I can, and I have prospects for some great supplemental income! Kaiya got accepted into a new charter school of the arts here, and she has REALLY blossomed. And, probably most importantly, I have made some very dear friends in all this. Ones that I correspond with in emails, or interact with on Facebook. They have seen our lives and how I am working to do better. I have suspended my quest for my Associate in Arts degree for the moment, and will be taking Certified Administrative Medical assistant classes in the spring. I qualified to take this program for free through the continuing education department at the college. It will be a step up . . . from there I can get a job in Medical Assisting, and may even add on to this with Pharmacy Tech or Medical Coding and Billing. It will enable me to pick a better job, one that I can take care of us with, and not have a constant worry about the future. I chose this route because I would be employable within a few months, which is more of a priority at the moment. Eventually I will go back for my degree . . . but the best thing about starting this way is, I KNOW I can do it.

Yeah. We're just a bunch of selfish, greedy, mean ol' conservatives. Mmm hmm.

There's a time and a place for welfare and social programs that help those in need. We believe in those safety nets for people who truly need them. But when safety nets turn into a way of life, the American dream is destroyed. Plain and simple.

Conservatives are right about the idea of offering a hand up to people in need, rather than just providing a handout to anyone that has a freaking hand. We realize that entitlement programs, and the thought processes behind them, keep more people down and out than enrich and empower them. Conservatives believe in the spirit and the strength of people over what the government can dole out to them. Conservatives believe in the tenacity and resilience and the amazing potential of individuals like Leslie and the readers who volunteered to help her.

And we're right about this.

CHAPTER 4

First Amendment Protections Extend to All Americans, Not Just Those with Whom We Agree

One day, we received a brief e-mail that perfectly represented the hate mail we get on a regular basis. It read, "This will be short and sweet. You are the most vile human beings. You disgust me and I hope we can someday rid our country and our planet of backswamp scum like you."

Yikes.

We replied to his message to ask, "Do you have a specific complaint or do you just hate us and wish us silenced in general?" And his response? "I'll go with the latter."

At least he was honest, right?

This is pretty typical of the kind of vitriol we experience regularly. These folks aren't the least bit shy about their disdain for our right to free speech. They're loud and proud about the fact that when it comes to the First Amendment, they'd just as soon have it only apply to those with whom they agree.

Conservatives are right to believe that no matter who you are, no matter what you think, no matter what ideology you subscribe to, you are free to speak your mind. We're right to reject attempts by the Left to silence us. We're right to con-demn the stifling of free speech by those who disagree with us and want us censored.

Liberals have accused us Chicks of being racist, intolerant, homophobic, classist, women-hating bigots. And we're not exaggerating—we've been called those things and worse. But the reality is that the liberals who demand acceptance and tol-erance for their beliefs and behaviors are often the same people who inundate us with unbelievably hateful Facebook messages, site comments, tweets, and e-mails suggesting in no uncertain terms that we should just stop talking altogether. We've received death threats with descriptive diatribes about how we should be maimed and tortured for daring to express our conservative beliefs. At our radio gig, our sponsors have received complaint letters for allowing us to endorse them. Our website has been systematically hacked on numerous oc-casions by liberals attempting to silence us. The truth is that many liberals are some of the *least* tolerant people around. They'd like nothing more than for conservatives to not have a voice at all and simply stand down. *Especially* female conser-vatives. We really irk them. (If you don't believe us, just ask Bill Maher, Ed Schultz, and David Letterman.) It kills them that we exist.

And you know what? *We freaking love that.* Their intoler-ance has made us louder and prouder than ever. It's that whole "nobody puts Baby in the corner" thing. Our skin has grown several extra layers since becoming the Chicks in early 2009. We've grown tough, because we know we're right. And con-servative women *have* to be extra tough, because we're fight-ing the happy-hippie, hand-holding liberals who have the media in their back pockets—which means that they get cover while beating us up, and face no accountability whatsoever.

FREE SPEECH TOLERANCE FROM OUR
WALL OF SHAME!

There's never a lack of fodder in our Facebook spam folder, and one morning back in 2014, we woke up to this gem on our timeline from a man named Jim:

You've just been reported, Bimbos. The FBI will be notified next. This goes way beyond free speech.

Jim followed his comment with another:

Just wanted you racist blond bimbos to know that I'm reporting this sight to Facebook.

We loved how Jim was on our Facebook page and planned to report our "sight" to Facebook. That was rich. We also thought it was hilarious that he had sinister plans to notify the FBI about us as well. As if they don't already know about us, in addition to the White House, the IRS, *and* the NSA. *As if.*

We look at our computers, wave, and smile to the NSA on a daily basis, Jim. But thanks for playing.

We have to be tougher still, because we're fighting against the conservative stereotype, too. We're not all homemakers who are barefoot and pregnant in the kitchen making sandwiches for our husbands. We're not waiting for a man's permission to speak. When liberals stereotype conservative women as fitting into that tiny, ridiculous box, we rather enjoy doubling down and fighting back against liberal censorship.

LIBERAL CENSORSHIP IN SCHOOLS

Liberals often squawk about coexistence and tolerance of others' viewpoints. They paint conservatives as bigots who reject differing opinions and lifestyles. But who's really censoring whom here?

Back in 2013 during the college commencement season, Kevin Hassett of the American Enterprise Institute wrote an op-ed in the *Miami Herald* about how college campuses shun conservative speakers. After researching the top one hundred universities and fifty liberal arts colleges, he found that "it [is] becoming increasingly apparent that conservative speakers aren't welcome on college and university campuses." The numbers were pretty staggering. No Republican official spoke outside of his or her home state. No conservative speakers were invited to speak at Ivy League school commencements, and no conservative elected officials spoke outside of the South. Only three identifiably conservative speakers were represented at the top 50 colleges and only 12 at the top 100 universities, compared to 69 identifiably liberal speakers. Sixteen speeches were given by Obama administration officials.[1]

Hassett concluded that our institutions of higher education—which are supposed to be places of expanded thought and open-minded places of learning—are actually some of the "most polarizing institutions in our society. Students who pass through them are remarkably well-prepared to join our uncivil political discourse."

These are *universities*, y'all. The places where we're sending our young adults to supposedly *expand* their minds, their horizons, and their viewpoints. Turns out that they're instead being molded and shaped into liberal drones who are essentially preprogrammed to believe that free speech only applies to fellow liberal drones. These are the same individuals who get pissed off when other students hand out things like United States Constitutions on Constitution Day.

No seriously. That happened.

ISN'T IT IRONIC?

If you can't believe that liberal censorship is a problem in public schools, get a load of this. Back in September 2013, the country celebrated Constitution Day. And even though there wasn't much fanfare, a kid named Robert Van Tuinen, a student at Modesto Junior College in California, decided to celebrate by passing out copies of our wonderful Constitution.

Pretty cool, if you ask us.

But school officials at Modesto didn't think it was cool at all. In fact, those school officials advised Van Tuinen that school policy required him to stop handing out copies of the Constitution.[2] If he wanted to pass out literature, he could only do so in a "designated free speech zone." Apparently, on a lot of college campuses now, your Constitutional right to free speech is limited to tiny little free speech "zones." That is, we're guessing, unless you're handing out free condoms or information on guilt-free abortions. In those cases, we wouldn't be the least bit surprised if your designated "zone" gets a hell of a lot bigger. But we digress.

Back to those pesky campus rules. In order to practice his Constitutional rights in that little designated zone on campus, Van Tuinen would have had to "obtain permission at least five days in advance." And he's allotted a total of eight hours a semester to exercise said First Amendment rights on his own college campus. You know, in that designated little "free speech zone." This is after going through the hoops to *get* the permission, and not even being guaranteed to be *granted* permission. Van Tuinen

HONORING AMERICA IN AMERICAN SCHOOLS MAY OFFEND NON-AMERICANS NOW. JUST FYI.

Our blood boiled over what happened in a Northern California high school—when in February 2014, the Ninth Circuit Court of Appeals ruled that it was completely and totally legal for an American high school to ban American flag T-shirts *in America* on Cinco de Mayo (which, in case you didn't know, is *not* an American holiday at all).[3]

A three-judge panel on the Ninth Circuit Court of Appeals ruled that the high school acted *appropriately* when they demanded that students wearing patriotic clothing turn it inside out so that it wouldn't offend Mexican students celebrating Cinco de Mayo. At an American high school. Again . . . *in America*. Which begs the question, can you imagine living in Mexico and being offended that Mexicans might wear patriotic Mexican clothing on the Fourth of July? Because if you can imagine that happening, you're living in a world that doesn't involve a lot of reality.

The court justified this completely absurd decision by saying that the school was concerned about potential violent disturbances resulting from angry Mexicans. That makes our blood pressures even more sky-high. The fact that it's completely discriminatory for the school to assume Mexican kids would get violent over patriotic American clothing notwithstanding, if students of Mexican descent *were* to get violent with kids for wearing American shirts *in America*, then they should be expelled. Period. You discipline the kids who incite the violence. What they did in Northern California was basically the same as punishing the kid who ate his vegetables because the kid next to him threw his vegetables on the floor. This isn't brain surgery, folks. It's common sense. We're right about this.

Again, this is *America*. Right? It still is, right? Where the First Amendment includes the right of self-expression, and where common sense would dictate that expressing one's love of country would easily fall under that, right? Because crap like this makes us really shake our heads and wonder.

did the math on this, and if everyone in the student body decided to make use of this little designated free speech zone, it would equate to two and a half minutes per student, per semester.[4] How's that for some American constitutional freedom, huh? Being the resourceful and educated young man that he is, Van Tuinen filed a lawsuit because he saw this as a violation of his First Amendment rights. Because it totally freaking was. And not just because we Chicks say so. In February 2014, Van Tuinen settled with Modesto Junior College to the tune of $50,000, and the school agreed to revise its speech codes.[5]

But let's be fair and get away from college campuses for a minute. If you're a conservative living in America, you're pretty well aware that most college campuses in this country are liberal mind-control camps. But once a young adult gets out into the real world, all of that liberal indoctrination and the desire to squelch the free speech of others starts to fade away, right?

Wrong.

LIBERAL INTOLERANCE: BEYOND THE CLASSROOM

Censorship of conservatives doesn't just happen at the institutional level. It happens beyond the classroom, and it happens with adults as well. Recently, a study was done by George Washington University that found that liberal people using the Internet are less tolerant than conservative web users are. The same study also showed that "22 percent of liberals have ended digital relationships, whatever they are, because somebody disagreed with them politically. For conservatives the number is 15 percent."

In other words, liberals are total babies when it comes to dealing with viewpoints other than their own. And since they corner the market on our American media, our educational system, and our pop culture—since they basically drive the narrative in this country—that should concern all of us. Protection of our First Amendment rights should be everyone's first concern. Consider, for example, the White House's attempt to silence conservatives by encouraging people to report those who might be spreading "disinformation" about Obamacare to flag@whitehouse.gov. Or Obama's "Organizing for America" website's "Attack Watch" program, set up to counter "someone who misrepresents the truth."[6] Or the same group's "Truth Team" also created to "fight back with facts against myths and lies on the issues that matter to us."[7] When our own president asks our fellow citizens to send e-mails about those they believe are "spreading disinformation," that is a problem.

. . . .

When our own president asks our fellow citizens to send e-mails about those they believe are "spreading disinformation," that is a problem.

. . . .

It should be pretty obvious at this point that the last thing liberals are is tolerant. They're not looking for healthy debate, because that makes them desperately uncomfortable. They want conservatives to shut up. We've experienced this first-hand as Chicks on the Right, by way of all of those threatening messages and hacking attempts. And that's the difference between us and them—we believe wholeheartedly in their right to insult us and disagree with us. They can scream at the top of their lungs that we are racist, intolerant, bigoted, homophobic, classist, ageist (that was a new one for us, too) jerks. They're wrong, but it's their prerogative to say what they want to say, because that's what the First Amendment is all about.

We respect that right, and we'll fight for them to be able to have it, no matter how wrong or misguided they are.

And the more they call for us to be quiet, the more we're going to turn it up to eleven.

BUT WAIT—CONSERVATIVES AREN'T BLAMELESS HERE!

Conservatives hurt their own cause when they make demands to shut down Bill Maher or other liberal media personalities simply because they speak their minds (however warped those minds might be). We think Bill Maher is one of the most reprehensible creatures on television, but he's got every right to be on television if there's an audience who wishes to see him there, and he's got every right to be a reprehensible creature who speaks his reprehensible mind. Conservatives need to stop trying to imitate the liberals' game by trying to shut him down.

We believe in God and are Christians, but we don't feel the need to tailor our political arguments and positions around scripture and Bible verses. We prefer to use data, facts, and the Constitution to make our points.

We've faced intolerance of our views by *fellow conservatives* as well. We've been criticized by fellow conservatives for what we wear, how we sit, the way we talk. When we express more flexibility on some issues than other conservatives would like, we're immediately labeled as RINOs or we're told we're not "real" conservatives. We're told we're not conservative enough, not Christian enough. That's nonsense. It's one thing to disagree on an issue, but it's entirely another to attempt to delegitimize our conservatism simply because we have a different viewpoint on a single topic, or because we wear shorts or say, "OMG."

Conservatives are often guilty of preaching in order to make their points, which is incredibly ineffective when dealing with people who are not religious. We believe in God and are Christians, but we don't feel the need to tailor our political arguments and positions around scripture and Bible verses. We prefer to use data, facts, and the Constitution to make our points. Atheist, agnostic, or otherwise nonreligious conservatives exist, and it's to our detriment to exclude them from the conversation. When the religious right preaches their case instead of stating it, they automatically turn away people who might otherwise be interested potential conservatives. They should know better than anyone that they should judge not, lest they themselves be judged.

We're right to call out fellow conservatives when they forget to practice what they preach.

THE GREAT FACEBOOK DEBACLE OF 2013

One day, back in January 2013, we woke up in the morning to discover that Facebook had locked Miriam out of our account, due to a "content violation." Rumors were already floating around the interwebs that Facebook was interfering with or completely shutting down conservative pages, so we went into full DEFCON red-alert mode, and decided to publicize the crap out of what was happening. The content violation, incidentally, was due to the fact that we'd posted an update which read, "Jay Carney can kiss my assular area" along with a link back to the full story at our website. Despite the fact that there are entire Facebook pages dedicated to killing Sarah Palin and others that proudly state that the Virgin Mary should have aborted Jesus, apparently suggesting that Jay Carney kiss our assular area is frowned upon. And a pop-up window on Facebook confirmed that they'd removed the *incredibly offensive violating content.*

After that pop-up came another informing us that in order to keep our account in "good standing," we needed to "remove any remaining content on [our] account that violates the Facebook terms."

Another screen showed that this was our *second* violation, and that a third would result in being banned from Facebook entirely. But since Amy Jo still inexplicably had access, we alerted our Facebook community (around eighty thousand people strong at that time), and sent messages to our friends in the blogosphere who we thought could help spread the word about what was happening.

Word started to travel. Some of our most faithful followers even started a new page called, "Save the Chicks from being banned from Facebook!" And while we were fairly certain that the many trolls who we consistently called out on our website and Facebook page likely banded together to "report" our page as often as they could, resulting in us being on some sort of automatic watch-list via Facebook's algorithms, we were determined to draw as much attention to this silencing attempt as we could. And that's when things really got interesting.

Just a couple of hours after we'd alerted our followers of what was happening, Todd Starnes of Fox News Radio picked up the story, and we received a phone call from him asking for details. Todd said he'd be writing a column about us, and sure enough, just a couple of hours later, there we were, two complete dorks, smiling broadly on the Fox News website. Our names were out. We were suddenly a national story. And it didn't stop there. We were featured on *The Blaze*, radio interview requests started pouring in, and even Whoopi Goldberg gave us a mention on *The View*.

And the best part? In spite of all of liberals' efforts to shut us down and trip up the Facebook algorithms and silence us, our following skyrocketed. We gained thirty thousand new followers practically overnight. Our traffic on the website exploded. And Facebook apologized to us, publicly, via the media outlets that were covering the story.

The moral of that story? When you're being silenced, speak louder. Turn it up to eleven. It's your right to have a voice. Liberals might have the upper hand in the mainstream media, but that doesn't mean they have the only hand. Speak up, speak loud, and do what you need to do to be heard. Because you're right. That was our takeaway from that life-changing experience.

That, and of course one of our favorite sayings: *Suck it, trolls.*

CHAPTER 5

Political Correctness Is Stupid

Remember back in the day, when people watched movies like *Blazing Saddles*, and TV shows like *All in the Family* and *In Living Color*, and we could laugh at those decidedly politically incorrect shows, and then go on with our lives and not act like a bunch of perpetually offended hosebeasts simply because Archie Bunker said something inappropriate? Remember when people weren't constantly walking on eggshells to avoid offending someone?

Good times.

It's different now. An *All in the Family* script wouldn't even reach a producer's desk in this day and age, because of this paralyzing fear that exists now of offending people. Unfortunately, it's not a baseless fear—the backlash from the political-correctness police can be intense. Those who dare to stray from the liberal script risk mockery, lawsuits, and even job loss. As a result, we've become so freaking afraid of offending someone or of hurting someone's feelings, that we're becoming mindless drones who, if liberals have their way, will only be capable of engaging in robotic, sterile interactions with one another.

It is right to challenge the PC world. You know why? Because political correctness is gay and retarded and all of those other adjectives we used to be freely allowed to say without being os-tracized. Take that, liberals (and hypersensitive conservatives).

George Carlin did a great bit about the "Seven Words You Can't Say on Television," warning that political correctness threatened free speech. He said, "It's left-wing paternalism. Years ago, we all got to expect that censorship would come from the right wing, but to expect it from the left wing—from the politically correct people on the campuses—that caught me by surprise."[1]

But it shouldn't have caught him by surprise. Liberals preach tolerance as if it's their job, but their efforts produce damaging zero-tolerance policies, cause people to mangle the English language in order to avoid imagined offense, hide truly offensive meanings behind pleasant-sounding words, and bully people in college and in the workplace into submission. Even acts of kindness and chivalry are seen as offensive now.

The world has officially gone mad.

Case in point.

ZERO TOLERANCE!

In January 2013, a school in Pennsylvania accused a five-year-old kindergartner of being a terrorist, because she told her classmate she was going to shoot her with her pink Hello Kitty soap-bubble gun. The school suspended the little girl for making a "terroristic threat."[2]

After the parents of the girl tried to reason with school officials, the punishment was reduced to two days' suspension and charges reduced from terror threats to merely "threatening to harm another student." Because as we all know, toy guns that blow soapy bubbles are very, very harmful.

And the kicker? The little girl didn't even have the toy gun with her when she apparently threatened the other child with *terror*. Still, her teacher saw fit to call her out in front of the whole class and tell everyone that police might get involved with the case. This reduced the five-year-old to tears.

Zero-tolerance policies are sweeping the nation's schools, such that stories like the Hello Kitty gun one are commonplace. It's why kids are suspended for biting their Pop-Tarts into the shape of guns, and they're suspended for sexual harassment if they dare to show harmless affection to another student. Because of our fear of political incorrectness, we've completely lost the ability to apply common sense to everyday occurrences.

LIBERAL MANIPULATION OF LANGUAGE

But it's not just zero-tolerance policies that are eating away at our culture and dumbing down our schools. It's the constant manipulation of the English language by well-intentioned but completely idiotic people who obsess over common words that could potentially hurt someone's feelings.

Consider, for example, that the term "illegal immigrant" was removed from the Associated Press style guide.[3] We're talking about the largest news-gathering outlet in the world here, and they removed the term "illegal immigrant" because they believed it "dehumanizes those it describes" and they found it to be "linguistically inaccurate."

The Associated Press apparently had "years of controversy over the term." Years of controversy over a term that accurately describes an immigrant who enters the country illegally. The Associated Press decided they didn't want to "label" people; instead, they only wanted to label behavior. Well guess what, AP! The people you're so desperately afraid of offending *illegally immigrated*. That was the behavior. *Hello*.

There are countless other examples, in addition to the AP's decision to discontinue the use of the term "illegal immigrant." Everyone remembers when Janet Napolitano, former head of

Homeland Security, suggested referring to acts of terror as "man-caused disasters."[4] Or when our own government decided to refer to Nidal Hasan's act of terror at Fort Hood as "workplace violence."[5]

In early 2014, the IRS referred to the penalty for failing to have health insurance coverage as a "shared responsibility payment."

This is becoming standard practice for the Left. If something they believe in sounds even remotely distasteful, then instead of owning the reality of their idea or policy or belief or value, they simply assign it a new name—something warm and fuzzy—so that low- and no-information leftists will continue to toe the party line, often oblivious to what they're actually supporting.

Considering how indefensible much of their ideology is, it's no wonder liberals want to hide behind soft, kind-sounding words. Talking about "women's bodily autonomy" sounds a whole lot better than talking about abortion. Spending becomes "investing." Raising taxes is called "redistribution of wealth" or "social justice." More recently, job losses occurring as a result of Obamacare were described as an avoidance of "job lock." You're not unemployed; you're liberated from work. New tax hikes? Those are just "increased revenues." Punishing the wealthy for their success by demanding more of their hard-earned money is just making sure they pay their "fair share."

. . . .

Considering how indefensible much of their ideology is, it's no wonder liberals want to hide behind soft, kind-sounding words.

. . . .

One of our favorites? The state of Maryland refers to its food stamp program's EBT card as an "Independence Card."[6]

What exactly are the cardholders independent from? Maybe it's that job-lock thing.

How do these word manipulations help anything? Here's a hint. They don't.

YOUR COMPLIMENTS ARE OFFENSIVE (IF I DON'T LIKE YOU)

Earlier we mentioned George Carlin's surprise at the rampant political correctness on college campuses. Not terribly long ago, the U.S. Justice Department sent a memo to all colleges that receive federal funding that outlines a new policy for sexual harassment prevention and punishment, and instead of a set of standards or a committee determination on what constitutes sexual harassment or "offensive speech," people can decide by themselves that they're offended by something someone else says, and the offender must be punished.[7] Just like that. Colleges have to suspend whoever is accused of being offensive without any hearing, without any investigation, without getting their side of the story. If they're accused, they're guilty. *In America.*

So if a dude says, "Oh—I like your new haircut" to a chick, and the chick doesn't particularly like that dude for whatever reason, she can claim that he objectified and offended her. That's all it takes to destroy that dude's record or career.

And we're not just talking sexual harassment. We're talking *anything* that might offend *anyone* for *any* reason.

This is what we mean when we say that if liberals have their way, we'll all end up living in a society where we act like robots. We will be so deathly afraid of offending one another that we'll just stop expressing ourselves altogether. We'll hide what we're reading, we'll avoid simple flirtation, and we'll bite our tongues and measure every word before speaking. This is apparently the kind of America liberals want.

We Chicks worked at a company several years ago where if we left for lunch, we were in danger of returning to find that our CFO had left hilariously inappropriate websites up on our computers as a joke. You know what we did? We laughed. We loved the practical jokes, the harmless flirtations, and the camaraderie with him and the other senior leaders. Because that's what made it fun to work there—people were free to be silly, and when it was time to be professional, we were. People with common sense, who are reasonable and who can understand the difference between harassment and harmless play, apparently are being outnumbered by liberal drones who *want* the sterile environments where no one ever cracks a smile for fear of it being misinterpreted.

FAIRY TALES ARE OFFENSIVE

Political correctness has already managed to warp childhoods, forcing some poor kids to grow up in that sterile world. There are liberal parents who are so keen on protecting their precious, special snowflakes from anything remotely frightening that they avoid some of the old fairy-tale classics that we grew up enjoying. As many as one in five parents have eliminated Snow White and Rapunzel from their kids' reading repertoires, and nearly half refuse to share the classic story of Rumpelstiltskin because of the kidnapping and execution themes.[8] The story of Goldilocks? That promotes stealing—so that's out, naturally.

A survey conducted of two thousand parents revealed that over half said they didn't care for the story of Cinderella, because it featured a woman doing housework all day. *For real.*

Can we get a show of hands here of those who know these stories, grew up reading them, and are somehow able to function, despite being exposed to the *horrors* of these *terrifying tales*?

We can pretty much guarantee you that the people who

refuse to read these classics to their kids are liberals, because they're the same sorts of people who suggest and employ zero-tolerance policies that defy common sense.

This kind of crap will simply result in more completely helpless, dependent, entitled people who cannot function like normal humans because they've been programmed to be afraid of everything and believe that only the government can take care of them. This is the poison of the liberal mind-set.

Conservatives are right to not get their panties in a wad about harmless humor or silly pranks. We're right to scoff at political correctness, because human beings are meant to laugh and not walk on eggshells with one another. Despite political correctness's best efforts, common sense isn't dead—it still lives in the conservative world.

CHIVALRY IS OFFENSIVE

We Chicks would hate to think that chivalry is dead, but if politically correct liberal feminists have anything to say about it, it's inevitable. To those bitchy harpies, it's simply not politically correct to hold a door open for a woman, apparently, because *feminism* and *woman power*. Or something.

Conservatives shouldn't worry for one second about offending liberal feminists. If some chick yells at a guy for holding a door open for her, citing her feminism and her strength and independence as the reason, the guy shouldn't be dissuaded. He should realize that he's a great guy, and if he doesn't already have one, he should find himself a nice conservative girl who appreciates some good old-fashioned chivalry, and then thank his mom for raising him right.

Chivalry does not equal sexism, contrary to popular feminist-wackjob belief. We're perfect examples of chicks who are professional career women, financial breadwinners in our families, and who still enjoy feeling cherished and taken care of by our husbands. Yet some feminists would claim that we're victims of "benevolent sexism." A term born in the mid-1990s, benevolent sexism is a "subjectively positive orientation of protection, idealization, and affection directed toward women that, like hostile sexism, serves to justify women's subordinate status to men."[9]

Here are some examples of benevolent sexism: Men opening doors for women. Men helping women carry shopping bags. Men offering to drive long distances. Men saying they "cherish" women. And the examples are not limited to men. Women are apparently guilty of benevolent sexism against themselves, too. We say "Hey, guys!" to a group that includes both sexes. We call ourselves "chicks," which according to the Society for the Psychology of Women, is a "blatant act of sexism."

In the *Psychology of Women Quarterly*, authors Julia Becker and Janet Swim said, "Women endorse sexist beliefs, at least in part, because they do not attend to subtle, aggregate forms of sexism in their personal lives." See, we're just not *attending* to all the sexism. Apparently these groundbreaking studies should be making us question what sorts of sexist jerks we married, what with all of their compliments and helpfulness and whatnot. *Damn them* for driving us places and carrying heavy things for us. Those selfish, sexist jerks.

. . . .

Apparently these groundbreaking studies should be making us question what sorts of sexist jerks we married, what with all of their compliments and helpfulness and whatnot. *Damn them* for driving us places and carrying heavy things for us. Those selfish, sexist jerks.

. . . .

What people who get all bajiggity about benevolent sexism always seem to forget is that context is important. Intent is important. And some of this benevolent sexism research crap is simply taking things too far.

The solution to real sexism isn't getting offended by well-meaning compliments or genuine offers to be helpful. How does it help society for men to be shamed when they hold a door open and admonished that the woman can open it herself? Too many feminists discourage simple politeness because they're so busy misplacing their outrage.

Many liberal feminists are so busy being offended, so hypervigilant in their quest to find things to be outraged about, that they're incapable of accepting simple acts of kindness without suspicion or of enjoying the sweetness of traditional chivalry. And if you're a dude who wants to compliment them on their appearance? Well, you clearly have a death wish.

Research published by *Social Psychological and Personality Science* claimed that women like us, who don't get our panties in a twist over having doors held open for us, must have a high sense of entitlement, which the same study said is a "core facet of narcissism." It suggested this entitlement translated into beliefs that women need to be protected by men and that women are naturally good caretakers versus CEOs.

That's ridiculous. We think women make fantastic CEOs *and* good caretakers. We think women can do either or *both*, because women are freaking awesome. We don't need political correctness to prove that.

BAN "BOSSY"!

In March 2014, Facebook COO Sheryl Sandberg, Girl Scouts of the USA, and numerous Hollywood elites (and disappointingly Condoleezza Rice as well) decided to add a new word to the list of politically incorrect terms. They launched a campaign to ban the word "bossy." The Ban Bossy campaign website read as follows:

> When a little boy asserts himself, he's called a "leader." Yet when a little girl does the same, she risks being branded "bossy." Words like bossy send a message: don't raise your hand or speak up. By middle school girls are less interested in leading than boys—a trend that continues into adulthood. Together we can encourage girls to lead.

Sandburg, Rice, Beyoncé, and others in the Perpetually Victimized Brigade were convinced that the word "bossy" holds females back, so they demanded that it be stricken from the American lexicon. Pretty bossy of them, really. And perplexing that the irony escaped them.

Side note: Isn't there a saying about "sticks and stones" that applies here?

There's no scientific data to show that the word "bossy" discourages girls from becoming leaders. There's no evidence that the word "bossy" prevents girls from having high self-esteem, or from becoming successful women. One of the few statistics offered on the Ban Bossy website was that "between elementary and high school, girls' self-esteem drops 3.5 times more than boys'."[10] No scientific study was cited to support that claim, probably because (a) none exists and (b) it's impossible to quantifiably measure something as intangible as self-esteem.

The lack of scientific credibility notwithstanding, the Ban Bossy campaign also neglected to acknowledge that the word "bossy" isn't gender specific. Parents assign that description to sons and daughters who exhibit pushy or overly assertive behavior. The definition of the word "bossy" is "overly authoritative;

domineering."[11] It's not about girls and women; it's about a human behavior. To make this a gender-specific issue is absurd. And, frankly, kinda sexist.

Men in leadership positions are called names every day with words rarely, if ever, used to describe women. But those men don't start ridiculous campaigns to ban words or whine that a word has damaged their self-esteem. They don't portray themselves as victims. That's what was also ironic about the Ban Bossy campaign. It was spearheaded by women of influence and power, who should've been holding themselves up as examples of how little the word "bossy" affected them. They achieved greatness despite being called bossy, and perhaps even because of it. They were determined to excel, and chose to be leaders, and they weren't about to let a silly adjective stop them. Why wasn't that their message?

The Ban Bossy website included "Leadership Tips for Parents," which instructed parents to watch and critique movies and TV shows with their children, focusing on gender roles, stereotypes, and the objectification of women. Hilariously, Beyoncé was one of Ban Bossy's celebrity spokeswomen. And one of the discussion questions suggested for parents was how often an actor dresses "in fancy or revealing clothing."

If you've seen Beyoncé's video "Partition," released right around the same time as this Ban Bossy campaign, interestingly enough, in which she writhes around provocatively wearing next to nothing, you'd understand why our eyes rolled so hard. The lyrics include female-empowering statements such as "I want to be the girl he likes" and "He Monica Lewinsky'd all on my gown."

Side note: As Monica Lewinsky herself also pointed out in *Vanity Fair*, why didn't she say he "Bill Clinton'd" all on my gown? Does Beyoncé need a biology lesson?

PREFERRED GENDER PRONOUNS

We now live in a politically correct world where we are going to be expected to deal with "preferred gender pronouns" in the off chance that we encounter a transgender or genderqueer person whose gender isn't instantly determinable. In an article for *Slate*, J. Bryan Lowder suggests that if you're "trans-supportive," then you should really ask the person with whom you're engaged in conversation which pronoun gender he or she prefers, so that you don't offend him or her. Yeah—because *that* won't be potentially offensive at *all* (insert eyeroll here). And not only should you ask what pronoun is preferred, but further still, you should ask *multiple times* because "gender is now understood to be fluid."[12]

OMG.

If your gender is "fluid," then we kinda think you need to either man or woman up and *deal* with the fact that people are going to use traditional pronouns to describe you. This could be the most ridiculous thing for anyone to ever get upset about *ever*. In life, no matter who you are, you are going to get your feelings hurt by people, for a wide variety of reasons. If you can't deal with that very simple reality, then creating a brand new "preferred gender pronoun" is the least of your worries.

To the credit of the "moderately masculine gay man who tries to be a trans ally" who wrote the *Slate* column, he does point out, "Well-meaning people accidentally disrespect one another all the time. Ideally, those unintended slights are gently corrected, and everyone moves on."

We were so relieved to see that speck of common sense injected into an otherwise totally ludicrous column. And even more relieved when he concluded, "Expecting people to change something as basic and ingrained as grammar is actually kind of a big ask."

We Chicks know we have conservative transgender folks who follow us, because they have, at times, reached out to us via e-mail and we've had genuinely lovely conversations. We have *mad respect* for them, knowing that on top of just dealing with the fact that they don't feel like they've got the right body parts, they *also* don't identify with the majority of the LGBT community, which, for the most part, leans way to the left. They basically get attacked by *everyone*. Which is why we would be willing to bet money that the conservative transgender people who follow us think this preferred-gender-pronoun stuff is nonsense, too.

But, in case you're interested in learning preferred gender pronouns and how to use them and what all of the rules are, you're in luck. The Gay Straight Alliance for Safe Schools has created a chart of eight possible pronouns:

- he
- she
- ze
- e
- ey
- per
- hu
- they[13]

All you have to do is learn the subjective, objective, possessive, and reflexive forms of these, and you'll never offend anyone again! *Yay!*

Notice that Beyoncé was encouraging girls to be someone a man likes. Real empowering there, Beyoncé. This is the same Beyoncé, incidentally, who President Obama said "couldn't be a better role model" for his daughters. We're pretty sure it's easier to find scientific data that demonstrate harm to little girls' psyches from exposure to vulgar, hypersexualized celebrities than it is to find data on how damaging the word "bossy" is.

These Ban Bossy activists would do far more good for girls and women if they stopped focusing on semantics, and instead focused on how to help our kids develop actual leadership skills. It damages us all when a campaign showcasing women of influence recommends banning a word simply because it hurts their feelings.

Ban *stupid campaigns*!

THE PERPETUALLY OFFENDED VS. REAL SEXISM

It's impossible to please everyone or to treat everyone precisely the way they wish to be treated. The expectation that we should somehow know how a person might perceive our words or actions in advance is unreasonable. Accusations of benevolent sexism—added together with political correctness gone haywire—sterilize our interactions with one another, making it impossible to establish real connections with people in the Land of the Perpetually Offended. And worse, it dilutes the validity of *real* sexism.

While liberals are busying themselves creating new crap to be offended about, like this benevolent sexism nonsense, they're simultaneously engaging in some of the worst examples of *actual* sexism ever. We experienced this firsthand when we wrote our first column for the *Indianapolis Star* newspaper in August 2013. The column was about feminism and its warping by liberal feminist harpies. We drew comparisons between women who rely on men to provide for them and women who rely on the government. We discussed the War on Women narrative. We explained our idea of conservative feminism—that being a true feminist was about female strength and independence, personal responsibility and self-reliance. And at the top of our column? The *Indianapolis Star* included our standard headshot:

No big deal, right? It's common to include an author photo along with a column. But here's what happened. People who took issue with our column couldn't bear to simply argue our points—they had to mention our *appearance* in some way, referring specifically to that photo. Here is one of the comments we received:

If you think your well-put-together bottle-blonde good looks have had nothing to do with the fact that you're getting a lot of attention—well, but you know that. You see the types of women who make it on Fox News and conservative talk shows. You certainly saw the potential to carve out a niche as your own little Hoosier Ann Coulter/Monica Crowley act. (I like how you touch heads in your photo. Hot!)

And check out this one:

> Admit it—you follow the Chicks On The Right because they're a head turn away from making out. No substance.

And that was just the tip of the iceberg! There were countless similar backhanded compliments from men. Men who *clearly* thought that the only *possible* reason we'd achieved any level of success was because of how we look.

That's real sexism, folks. And so is this from Ketrick on Facebook:

> Why do self-hating broads on the right—who are presumably so religious—wear so much make-up? Isn't that whorish or is it all about altering your appearance to please the shallow doucher you call a loving husband?

And this from a group called Free Thought and Discussion: The Politics and Spirituality:

> Yes, all you blonde trophy wife bimbos go order your latest edition of 'How to be a proper brood mare' so that you can sit in your little book clubs and talk about how pathetic your marriage-life is.—ViP

And, of course, this from Eric:

> You whores look like the typical Scottsdale AZ c***s I see mindlessly driving around town in giant SUVs spending some dipsh*ts money in the middle of the day.
>
> Got bored spending without earning (wow you sound like the imaginary "liberal" you've made up) and decide to create a Facebook page pretending to know a G*D DAMNED thing about politics . . .
>
> Hope 'y'all' bleed to death you're next menstrual cycle =)

The above examples are just a small sampling of the kind of crap we conservative chicks receive on a regular basis. And these are from those tolerant, forward-thinking progressives. Nice, huh?

Liberals love to brand themselves as the folks who care about women. But that's only if you're another liberal. If you're a conservative woman, you're a "Koch-sucking slut." Or a whore or a c*nt.

There's benevolent sexism, which is nonsense made up by harpies who are perpetually offended by everything, even tender acts of chivalry, and then there's real sexism, like the kind we see from trolls. Apparently the "kindness" behind political correctness is only extended to those with whom they agree.

We'll take the guy who holds doors open for us over those sexist liberal losers any day of the week.

THE WORD "RETARDED," MIRIAM'S SON, AND HER UNCONVENTIONAL ATTITUDE

Miriam here. Conservatives are not exempt from falling prey to political correctness. For example, let's look at the word "retarded."

The word "retarded" has become a really big deal over the past decade or two. Over the last several years, entire movements have been created, dedicated to bringing an end to the casual use of this term, because, as the R-word organization states:

> The R-word hurts because it is exclusive. It's offensive. It's derogatory. Our campaign asks people to pledge to stop saying the R-word as a starting point toward creating more accepting attitudes and communities for all people. Language affects attitudes and attitudes affect actions. Pledge today to use respectful, people-first language.[14]

My older son is severely intellectually disabled, in addition to having cerebral palsy and being a quadriplegic. He has the intellectual capacity of a three-month-old. I would never use the word "retarded" derisively toward him or any other person with *actual* mental retardation. But the word is, for better or worse, part of my everyday slang vocabulary, and I've been known to call everything from hot-pink thigh-high boots to Miley Cyrus's latest shenanigans "retarded." I use it in the same way I use the word "gay," actually (and there's a campaign to stop everyone from doing that as well).[15] Since I love my son, and I love a lot of gay people, I obviously don't intend to disrespect them. They're just words that are part of the

American slang vernacular, and I've picked them up, as I might any other habit-forming term or phrase.

I understand completely why people take offense to the word "retarded" being used in a derogatory way about someone with an actual intellectual disability. But frankly, I'm tired of all of this political correctness. The perpetual offense that people take to words uttered by others who clearly do not mean offense by them has gotten out of control. *Of course* we should condemn those who use words to intentionally hurt and deride people with mental disabilities. But I just can't bring myself to accept that my calling Miley Cyrus's tongue acrobatics "retarded" is somehow an affront to my intellectually disabled son. There are miles and miles of distance between the meaning of the word "retarded" as it relates to a celebrity who acts like a ridiculous skank, and the meaning of the word "retarded" as it relates to someone with an actual intellectual disability. Interestingly, the official diagnosis of "retarded" is no longer even referenced in the most recent version of the *Diagnostic and Statistical Manual of Mental Disorders*, instead being replaced with "intellectually disabled."[16] The word "retarded" in the *DSM*, in fact, replaced "feebleminded" and "idiot" and "mentally subnormal" once *those* words were determined to be offensive. But do you see entire campaigns devoted to eliminating the word "idiot" from colloquial use? No—because people haven't just collectively decided, inexplicably, to be offended by it. You hear people throw around the word "idiot" everywhere—on TV, on the radio, to tease one another—and no one is having a fit over it. There is no "Ban the I-Word!" campaign. Yet for some reason, the word "retarded" has caused a complete uproar.

· ·

You hear people throw around the word "idiot" everywhere—on TV, on the radio, to tease one another—and no one is having a fit over it. There is no "Ban the I-Word!" campaign.

· ·

One day, when Amy Jo and I were on the air, I made reference to "retarded celebrities." I knew the instant the word escaped my lips that the calls and letters would pour in. Sure enough, they did. One mom with an intellectually disabled daughter wrote to tell me that using the word "retarded"—even when not directed at the "challenged population"—was hurtful. She said it was her job as a mom to stand with her child. She insisted that as long as adults continued to call things and people retarded, then we couldn't possibly expect our kids not to use that word against mentally challenged children. I disagree, because again, the meaning of the word "retarded" in today's slang has nothing to do with people who are genuinely intellectually disabled. More often than not, people who use the term colloquially, myself included, would never dream of being anything but kind and compassionate to people with disabilities. Intent matters. My younger son might hear me say that something Miley Cyrus does is "retarded," but he'll certainly never hear me say anything hurtful or demeaning toward a mentally challenged or otherwise disabled person.

And the word war doesn't stop there. It's apparently racist to say, "Let's call a spade a spade." During the Trayvon Martin / George Zimmerman case, we witnessed the media fighting about whether it was appropriate to use the word "cracker" in relation to white people. I can't even suggest that this whole issue is "low on the totem pole" of priorities for me without worrying that someone might take offense on behalf of American Indians. Seriously—could someone just provide a pocket handbook with a list of all the words that could potentially offend people? Because I can't keep up.

This hypersensitivity to the word "retarded" frankly offends me *on behalf of* intellectually disabled people like my own son. Why are we encouraging them to be wounded by words, particularly when the words aren't used derisively toward them? Why not raise our kids, disabled or able-bodied, to know the same adage we were taught ourselves—that sticks and stones may break our bones, but words can never hurt us?

It's an unconventional attitude, I suppose, for the mom of an intellectually disabled boy to have. But the bottom line is this: My lovely son, in addition to his other disabilities, has mental retardation. Miley Cyrus twerking with her tongue out is retarded.

There's a difference.

Instead of the campaigns against words and the handwringing over semantics, why don't we leave the hypersensitivity and manufactured outrage to the liberal left, where they've practically made it an art form? Conservatives are right to focus on more pressing matters than words. There's no reason for conservatives to fall into the trap of political correctness, which serves no purpose other than to complicate human interactions. We're better than that. And if we scoff at zero-tolerance policies and mock how the liberal left manipulates language to suit their causes, then we need to practice what we preach and not go on similar crusades to ban words that we've decided make us uncomfortable.

If there's anything we should ban, it's political correctness.

CHAPTER 6

We Have a Constitutional Right to Things That Go *Pew-Pew-Pew*

In early 2014, an anonymous tipster notified local police in Buffalo, New York, that a person was carrying a gun at a public elementary school. A dozen squad cars, a SWAT team, K9 units, a helicopter, and an armored vehicle showed up on the scene. The school was placed on lockdown. While all the kids were moved to the cafeteria, cops did a sweep of the school to make sure they were safe.[1]

The police arrested a guy named Dwayne Ferguson for carrying a gun illegally at the school. But here's the kicker: Ferguson is a well-known, local community activist who has been integral in pushing gun control in his community, and he's one of the dudes responsible for passing New York's SAFE Act.

So why would he have been carrying a gun around at an elementary school, you might ask? Well, he was at the school because he works there in the afternoons, and he had a gun on him because he says that he "carries a pistol." For which he apparently has a permit. Which is interesting, because that permit is about as valid as a cocktail napkin with "Me have a gun!" scribbled on it, ever since the state law *he helped pass* went into effect. Dwayne ostensibly understood that carrying a gun on school grounds was now considered a felony, so he of all people should have remembered to leave his gun locked up at home that day.

He must have been distracted when he was pounding the pavement trying to take other people's Second Amendment rights away from them. Funny how that works, isn't it?

Unlike Dwayne Ferguson, conservatives revere and appreciate the Second Amendment and believe that we have a right to bear arms. It's right for conservatives to want to protect the Second Amendment from being crapped on by the liberal machine. When liberals use tragedies like the shootings in Aurora, Colorado, and Newtown, Connecticut, for their own political agendas, conservatives are right to condemn them. We're right to kick up a fuss when law-abiding citizens are punished and penalized because of the acts of insane criminals. We're right to acknowledge that responsible gun ownership can actually make people safer, because we know that it's not the guns themselves that pull the triggers. Only idiots believe that guns go off by themselves, for crying out loud. *People* commit crimes. Not objects.

NEVER WASTE A TRAGEDY

Within the context of the gun control debate, liberals often justify their position of wanting strict gun control measures by demonizing the weapons themselves, instead of the real problem: the inherent evil that exists in the people who use them with malice. Even though the NRA's mission is to protect our Second Amendment rights, liberals make it a frequent target (no pun intended) because they are convinced that the guns themselves are the source of evil.

After the Newtown shooting in late 2012, filmmaker and

liberal poster boy Michael Moore wrote an op-ed about how he wanted everyone to be forced to look at pictures of the children who were riddled with bullet holes in that tragedy. He wanted the crime scene pictures to be released to the public. He thought if that happened—if people were exposed visually to sweet, innocent, five- and six-year-old children shot to pieces—the NRA would somehow cease to exist.

In his borderline-psychotic anti-NRA rant, Moore employed the Emmett Till story to make the case that Americans would simply scrap the whole Second Amendment thing if only we saw the bodies of lifeless children shot to death in Newtown.

If you're unfamiliar with the Emmett Till story, he was a fourteen-year-old black boy from Chicago who was murdered in cold blood for talking to a white woman while he was visiting his relatives in Mississippi back in 1955. His body was found and returned to his hometown of Chicago, and his mother not only insisted on having an open casket, but also insisted on photographs being taken of Emmett's body so that those photographs could be published in as many newspapers and magazines across the country as possible. She wanted everyone to see what the bigoted killers had done to her son.

Like Emmett Till's mother, the mother of Noah Pozner (a victim of the Newtown shooting) wanted an open casket for *her* son's funeral.[2] She wanted people to see "what guns did to her son" that horrible day in December 2012. As mothers, our hearts broke for her. We ached for all of the parents, the siblings, the grandparents—*everyone* and *anyone* who knew and loved the children of Newtown—and we continue to ache for them every time we think of what happened that day.

But Michael Moore didn't just ache for the victims. He used the tragedy to further his agenda that had been in place long before the shooting. He hates the NRA, and he's willing to use any circumstance to bring it down. Exploiting the nation's grief over Newtown, he drew a correlation between Till's photo and photos of Newtown's children in order to paint NRA supporters as the equivalent of white supremacists.

He even made the open threat to the NRA at the end of his rant: "Pack your bags, NRA—you're about to be shown the door. Because we refuse to let another child die in this manner. Got it? I hope so. All you can do now is hope no one releases those photos."

To Michael Moore—and many other liberals—the *NRA* was actually responsible for killing those children. Not the guy who actually pulled the trigger, Adam Lanza, but every single one of the NRA's more than five million law-abiding members. It wasn't a human being who killed those children. It was an entire organization. Newtown provided yet another opportunity for yet another witch hunt for gun rights supporters.

Moore's rant is disturbing to us as mothers, yes, but also as rational, thinking, logical human beings who want our children to grow up in a world where there is a clear delineation between right and wrong. We want our kids to grow up in a world where there's a strong sense of personal responsibility, and where there is accountability for criminal activity, appropriate care for mental instability, and awareness of the existence of pure, unadulterated evil. We wish the world were different, but trying to ignore the presence of evil is naïve—and dangerous. Just as a cotton gin wasn't responsible for the death of Emmett Till, so a gun was not responsible for the deaths of the Newtown children. People were responsible for both. Evil people.

What haunts us about these two examples is not so much the calling for open caskets, not the pictures, not the *shock value*, per se. We understand the value of shaking people out of their desensitization and numbness to violence. Holy crap, we get that.

We really do. But we fear that gun control mania allows the real cause of shootings to go unrecognized and unchecked.

In his rush to show us what guns can do to little children's bodies, Michael Moore missed the root of the problem—the evil that destroys not just bodies but also souls. Evil, after all, is what lurked in Adam Lanza's soul and made him pull the trigger that fateful day. Evil was the catalyst for his actions, which resulted in the loss of twenty-seven innocent lives and his own suicide. While conservatives focus on trying to understand what causes the kind of evil mentality that prompts a person to go on a murderous rampage, jackasses like Michael Moore focus on the *tools* used by evil people to cherry-pick for their own selfish, messed-up agendas.

Tools are the low-hanging fruit for liberals, though. It's a hell of a lot easier to focus on tools than to look at how messed up we've become as a society—to get to root causes of why people become unhinged. It's easier to place blame on a thing that can be controlled, or an organization that promotes responsible use of that thing, rather than the person who was a raving, unfit-for-this-earth lunatic. It's way easier to focus on a mean ol' gun than on the evil of the person wielding it.

. . . .

Tools are the low-hanging fruit for liberals, though. It's a hell of a lot easier to focus on tools than to look at how messed up we've become as a society—to get to root causes of why people become unhinged.

. . . .

Moore assumed that there would be backlash to his rant, so he preemptively claimed that any outrage resulting from the publication of those gruesome photos would be "false outrage" and that seeing the slaughtered bodies of twenty children would force us to act immediately to rid the country of guns.

Nowhere in Moore's "editorial" did he talk about the 1.21 million kids that were murdered in 2008 alone via abortion.[3] Don't hold your breath waiting for liberals like Michael Moore to force folks into looking at photographic evidence of the carnage from abortion. In fact, liberals lose their freaking minds when you publish pictures of aborted human beings (which has always baffled us, because liberals don't think fetuses are human . . . so, why all the outrage?). And you know why? It's because Michael Moore and his liberal friends are cherry-picking wusses. Aborted children have nothing to do with the NRA, or guns, or his liberal agenda, so what does he care? It's just a *million* or so dead kids. But no *guns* were involved, so pfffft. Whatevs.

If Moore wants everyone to look at the violence of our society, then we say let's do it. Let's look at the real causes for said violence. Let's look at evil. Let's look at the *whys* and the *hows* and the root causes. Because we can tell you right now—it's not about the tools. If you zone in just on the tools, then you better be prepared to start cutting off the hands that strike or beat women every fifteen seconds in this country, too. And you should ban the spoons that made Michael Moore morbidly obese while you're at it.

That's how ridiculous the liberal argument against guns is. The problem isn't the hands. And it's not the spoons. And it's *not the guns*.

It's the evil.

One thing liberals have a problem understanding, but that conservatives comprehend quite well, is that you can't legislate

THE STUNNING HYPOCRISY OF HOLLYWOOD
HEAVYWEIGHT HARVEY WEINSTEIN

Early in 2014, big-shot Hollywood producer Harvey Weinstein proclaimed on Howard Stern's radio show that he was going to make a "big movie like a *Mr. Smith Goes to Washington*" with Meryl Streep and that it was going to destroy the National Rifle Association. In fact, his exact words were "We're going to take this head-on, and they're going to wish they weren't alive after I'm done with them."[4]

He told Stern that he'd never owned a gun and never would, and he went so far as to say that no one needs guns in this country. If you're not familiar with Weinstein's work, let us tell you something about him: he's responsible for executive-producing such movies as *Pulp Fiction*, *Reservoir Dogs*, *Kill Bill*, *Rambo*, and *Inglourious Basterds*. If you've seen any of those violent, gun-filled films, you will understand why we think that Harvey is a raging liberal Hollywood hypocrite.

A few days after his filmmaking threat to the NRA, Weinstein was called out for said hypocrisy and he addressed it, pledging that he "will no longer make movies with egregious violence." He went on to tell Piers Morgan, "I'm not going to make some crazy action movie just to blow up people, and exploit people." That's all well and good, until you remember that he's already made his $150 million fortune from crazy action movies full of gratuitous violence. How convenient for him to swear off violent movies now that he's in a position to ponder which of his mansions he should sleep in any given evening.

Harvey Weinstein doesn't really want a world without guns. For crying out loud, *guns have helped make him rich and successful.* Just go see one of his ridiculously violent movies and tell us otherwise. He just doesn't want *you* to have guns. This is typical liberal thinking. It's why antigun celebrities will do black-and-white PSAs about how guns are horrible weapons with minds of their own, yet they'll never give up their armed guards. And they sure as hell won't give up the gazillions of dollars they make while they're glorifying gun use in movies. The liberal gun-grabbing crowd hates guns, unless they're making money off of them. As always, what's good for them is never good for the rest of us.

evil. Conservatives know that evil and crazy exist, and neither of those things can be legislatively banned. Oh sure, you can legislate against evil acts. But evil people who mean harm against others will never be deterred by laws. Pretending that the problem is guns (the tool) is a lot easier than accepting that evil exists in the world, because it's a piece of cake to shriek for gun control. It's not quite as easy to demand evil control. There is no amount of legislation that will ever make evil people less evil. But you can be certain that if liberals *could* figure out a way to legislate evil, they'd find a way to tax it, too.

THE LIBERAL NARRATIVE OF THE INVISIBLE AR-15S

On September 16, 2013, Aaron Alexis, a lone gunman armed with a shotgun, shot and killed twelve people inside the Washington Navy Yard in Washington, DC. Several lamestream media outlets took to the airwaves to blame the shooting on an AR-15. For some reason, the AR-15 has become the liberal's go-to most hated gun du jour. It doesn't go bang-bang, but instead goes *pew-pew-pew*, and that really freaks liberals out, so naturally they want to ban it. They love banning stuff.

At the time, Piers Morgan was the self-appointed lead crusader against the AR-15. The problem with blaming the Navy Yard shooting on this particular weapon, though, is that the FBI confirmed that no AR-15s were used by the shooter, navy reservist Aaron Alexis. They further confirmed that a shotgun and two pistols were recovered, and that the gunman was not armed with an AR-15 at all, much to the dismay of blokes like Piers Morgan, who took to the airwaves immediately after the shooting to use it as a soapbox for his liberal antigun agenda.[5] Piers was convinced that if we just rid the world of those mean ol' AR-15s, the Navy Yard shooting wouldn't have happened at all.

But never mind that the FBI confirmed an AR-15 wasn't even used. Never mind that the shooter was mentally ill. Never mind that a person was actually behind the gun at all. Never mind all that. AR-15s *are bad and should be banned*. If you'd please just stick to the leftist narrative and move along, minions.

Nothing to see here.

The lamestream liberal media will always perpetuate the lies. And in the case of the evil AR-15, Piers Morgan was about as credible as actor Henry Winkler, who tweeted:

> ΛNOTHER shooting in WASH D.C. PLEASE America do nothing to promote gun control .because thats how we roll until we have all shot each other.

Right, Fonz. That's how we roll. We all just want to shoot each other. In fact, we believe that's precisely what the Second Amendment of the Constitution says. Verbatim. Mmmm hmmm.

What Piers Morgan and the Fonz forget is that liberals have already tried to legislate evil by creating "gun-free zones." The Navy Yard is one of those places. Aaron Alexis chose not to follow the rules the day he decided to walk into that gun-free zone with a gun. Criminals, by definition, usually don't follow the

PEARL JAM'S FRONT MAN WISHES
HARM TO GUN OWNERS

In an interview with Mark Richards, Eddie Vedder said that 90 percent of us in this country want more gun laws. Yeah. He said that out loud. Additionally, Eddie wants bad things to happen to people with guns. It's like punishment. So, you can imagine his delight when children get their hands on them.

"If I didn't have music to kind of at least get some of the aggression out or take the edge off, you wouldn't want me having a gun either. I get so angry that I almost wish bad things upon these people," Vedder said. "But I don't have to because it seems like they happen anyways. It seems like every week I'm reading about a 4-year-old either shooting their sister, their dad, their dog, their brother or themselves, because there's f**king guns laying around. But I guess it's 'fun.' "[6]

To quote the great and fictional Homer Simpson: "Rock stars—is there anything they don't know?"

rules that law-abiding citizens do. What happens when you set up law-abiding people in gun-free zones where they can't protect themselves from the bad guys who *don't* follow the rules?

Defenseless people get killed—thanks to liberal legislation.

THE SCHOOL MASSACRE THAT WASN'T

If not for conservative bloggers and conservative media outlets, it's entirely possible that we'd never hear about how often guns actually *save* people's lives. About a year after the Newtown school shooting, Americans witnessed another shooting at yet another school. As we watched the coverage on the news, we initially feared the worst. A lone gunman, prepared much like

Adam Lanza was and making no effort to conceal the fact that he was about to go on a rampage, walked into Arapahoe High School in Colorado ready to kill people. He was decked out with a bandolier containing shotgun shells, and he carried a pump-action shotgun, a machete, and a backpack that contained three Molotov cocktails. He was also in full-on tactical gear.[7] As Arapahoe county sheriff Grayson Robinson observed, "His intent was evil, and his evil intent was to harm multiple individuals."

The gunman shot seventeen-year-old Claire Esther Davis while presumably on his way to murder a teacher who kicked him off the debate team months earlier. The loss of one young woman that day was tragic, but the death toll could have been much worse. Instead, no one else was killed other than the gunman, Karl Pierson. He took his own life when he realized that an armed school resource officer was coming for him.

Sheriff Robinson stated, "We know for a fact that the shooter knew that the deputy was in the immediate area and, while the deputy was containing the shooter, the shooter took his own life." Had that deputy not been in the immediate area, and had he not been armed, and had he not run to the scene at that moment, more innocent lives would've been lost. It's as simple as that.

As conservatives, we believe that "gun-free zones"—common in schools—put law-abiding citizens into sitting-duck situations. Good people become open targets for criminals, wackjobs, and bad guys. You might as well put up a sign in these places that says, "Yoo-hoo, bad guys! No one will stop you! Over heeeeere!"

We don't suggest for a second that eliminating gun-free zones will eliminate mass shooting attempts. We're not naïve. But what happened at Arapahoe is proof that properly armed, law-abiding citizens can, in fact, save lives. It doesn't matter if it's AR-15s or handguns—the tools are irrelevant. Armed and skilled resource officers freaking *work*. And that's why we side with responsible conservatives who would like to see armed resource officers in our schools. After all, if it's acceptable for the president of the United States to have his daughters protected by armed guards, why not *our* kids?

FIGHTING FIRE WITH FIREPOWER

The hypocrisy of the Left on the gun issue is overwhelming. Conservatives are right to fight hard to protect the Second Amendment. We're right to support the NRA in its efforts to do just that. Liberals and some conservatives alike often decry the money spent by the NRA to lobby Congress, and while we're not fans of money doing all the talking on the Hill, we recognize that in order to play the game, we must fight fire with fire. And in DC, fire is money.

We Chicks are firm supporters of the NRA and of anyone who takes a stand to protect our Second Amendment rights. As gun owners, we know that the most important obligation we have is to protect our families and our homes. We also recognize that with the right to bear arms comes the responsibility to be well trained and well educated about proper use and handling of any firearm we own. We take this very seriously, and expect the same of others.

We know full well that we don't live in a perfect world, and that criminals who intend harm on others will find a way, with firearms or otherwise, to carry out their evil acts. Restricting gun ownership by responsible citizens as a measure to stop violent crime is pointless and dangerous. Conservatives are right to insist that when an evil criminal uses a weapon for an evil purpose, it's the evil criminal who should be dealt with—not the weapon.

CHAPTER 7

Skin Color Is Irrelevant

Back when George W. Bush was president, he was often lampooned as a monkey. We can't count the number of memes that paired a picture of him with a picture of a chimpanzee in a similar pose, similar outfit, and a dead-on George W. expression on its face. So-called journalists wrote articles about how George W. looked (and sometimes acted) like a monkey. The president of the United States was compared to a freaking *primate*, y'all, and that was apparently hilarious at the time.

Fast-forward a few years to when we Chicks post Obama cartoons in which he sports the same exaggerated facial features sketched in the George W. Bush cartoons. We're instantly branded as racists. Never mind that exaggeration is what cartoonists *do* in caricatures. Apparently if you don't believe that Obama is the best thing since sliced bread, you've got a problem with the color of his skin. Comparing a white president from Texas to a monkey is totally fair game. Because he's *white*. If you're making fun of a white guy, race isn't an issue. If you're making fun of a guy who has any pigment in his skin whatsoever? Race is *the* issue.

We conservatives are downright exhausted from talking about race. You know why? Because we don't give a crap about the color of anyone's skin. For crying out loud, we have a black president who was voted into office by a majority of people in this country. Twice. He was supposed to end the racial divide and be the Great Unifier. But the divide is greater than ever, and conservatives have been painted as racists simply for thinking Obama is a sucky president.

Even worse than being painted as racists without cause is the fact that we're expected to feel shame *simply for being white.* Race-obsessed professors shame students into believing that words like "uppity" are racist. Seminars are held to help teachers come to grips with their lack of "cultural competence."

Are there racists in this country? You bet. On both sides of the aisle. Liberals love to pretend that racism is solely a conservative problem, but it's often those same liberals who fixate on race. It's those same liberals who base every argument, every debate, and every conversation around the color of someone's skin—and you know what that means? *They* are the ones being racist. Yeah, we said it.

Most conservatives simply don't care about skin color, and we'd just as soon stop talking about it and start treating everyone as equals already. We recognize that liberal policies of affirmative action, the "soft bigotry of low expectations," and a racism-thirsty media keep racism alive in this country. The determination of liberals and Democrats to keep minorities in a perpetual state of victimhood has actually done far more damage to race relations than *actual* instances of racism.

Conservatives are right to call liberals out on the neverending charges of racism they levy, simply because we think the first black president couldn't lead himself out of a bathroom without a teleprompter.

Let's be crystal clear on this matter. We disagree with our president's ideology. If he were white, we would continue to disagree with it. It doesn't really get any simpler than that.

HAVE WE MENTIONED THAT THE GOP SUCKS AT MESSAGING?

Conservatives, however, need to recognize that we have a pesky messaging problem to contend with. Unfortunately, we don't have the stranglehold on the media that the Left does, so the narrative is driven by those who say that right-wingers hate anyone who isn't white. And when we are given the microphone, we're not the coolest of the bunch. In fact, we're like the nerdy dude with glasses who is super savvy about financial and national security topics, but is totally socially inept. The liberal-dominated media has spent the last few decades spoon-feeding minorities the tale that conservatives have forgotten about them, that we've discarded them, and that we just don't give a rat's ass about them. We're constantly on the defensive in the game of politics, instead of being on the offensive. And that's a really, *really* big problem for us. See the painful elections of 2008 and 2012 as evidence.

While Democrats are telling black and Hispanic folks, "Here's a bunch of free crap for you, because we really care about you!" we're busying ourselves telling people that they have to buck up, get off their asses, and actually work for stuff.

That's a much tougher sell, frankly. And when two PR machines are competing for voter love, the former sell is a lot sexier. Our job is a lot harder. Especially when we're constantly dealt the race card.

THE RACE CARD

Calling conservatives racist in an argument provides an easy out for liberals, because their arguments usually suck. Instead of engaging on ideas, a liberal throws down the race card, and the chance for any reasonable discussion ends there. Thoughtful, meaningful debate is impossible now that liberals whip out the race card as a nearly involuntary response to every argument.

Case in point. In 2013, we posted a joke on our Facebook page that read, "Please don't say 'firecracker.' We find this highly offensive. Please say 'fire white-American.' Thank you." In response to that joke, one of our followers commented, "I prefer 'person of pallor,'" which we loved so much that we posted it as a separate status update.

And then, along came Susi. She wrote the following on our wall:

> "This site just made me puke. You can now delete this post."

We responded:

> "And deny you the opportunity to post something this pithy, this insightful, this profound AGAIN? NEVER. We'll keep it up.—Mock"

Susi fired back:

> "Well good then. Keep that white on. You do so well with it."

And then:

> "You women really live up to your name. Wow it is no surprise why most of the world hates us. They think we are all racists like you. Unbelievable."

"Keep that white on"? What does that even mean?

We asked Susi if she was mad about the "people of pallor" thing, and how, exactly, she came to the conclusion that we are racists. This was her explanation.

> "I never labeled you racist until I read your posts. You convinced me."

Is it possible that she simply saw the name of our page, hates conservative women, is too miserable of a person to appreciate the humor of the "people of pallor" pun, and simply decided to crap on our wall without an *actual* point? We decided to try to find out.

> What post convinced you? Be specific. Was it the People of Pallor one? Because if you are offended by that, Susi—you have even less of a sense of humor than I gave you credit for. You're just like the liberal feminists we make fun of—humorless, perpetually offended, intolerable, miserable, hosebeasts who can't STAND

the fact that conservative women exist, and that we're happy.

Well, sorry to disappoint. But we do. And we are. ☺

Hey—what do you think about Ben Carson? And Mia Love? And Condi Rice? Just curious.

Susi didn't care for that question, and as we kept going back and forth a bit, trying to get her to offer evidence of her accusations, and correcting her spelling on something, she responded with this gem:

Here is a spelling you can correct if you would like. F*ck you you racist b*tch. Good bye.

We were a little bummed out that she caved so quickly. We were totally up for a longer quarrel, but Susi obviously couldn't handle truth or common sense or reality, so asking her to be specific about her accusations was pretty futile.

Side note: We didn't have the heart to tell her that she spelled "F*ck you you racist b*tch" correctly, so there was really nothing for us to fix on that point (unless you count the missing comma).

As Susi demonstrated quite well, the reason liberals use the race card so often is because it eliminates the need for them to actually *think*.

Conservatives know this, because we actually *do* think.

PAPER IS RACIST

Anne O'Connor, an "early years consultant" has questioned the use of white paper in classrooms. She and other "equality experts" also worry about the "negative message" being sent to toddlers in nursery school when they see toy witches wearing black, because it's racist.[1] They'd prefer that witches have pink hats. Even more ridiculous, O'Connor also says that children should be provided paper that spans "the full range of flesh tones" because then it would properly reflect the diversity of the human race.

It's freaking paper we're talking about here, y'all. And while Anne O'Connor only seems to be inflicting her wisdom on nursery schools in the UK, her progressive way of thinking is common here in the United States as well. Anne has outlined a set of guidelines for nursery schools to follow, the purpose of which is to help toddlers avoid racial bias. Because you know how racially insensitive two-year-olds can be. Those little jerks. And you know where those guidelines apparently come from? The multiculturalistic approach to education developed right here in the United States. *Awesome!*

Apparently, Anne O'Connor and her ilk believe that it is up to nursery school teachers to help toddlers "unlearn" any discriminatory feelings they may have about skin color. They believe teachers should be "economical with the truth" when they are asked by their students what their favorite color is, and in fact answer "black" or "brown."

We wish we were making this up.

O'Connor said, "People who are feeling defensive can say 'well there's nothing wrong with white paper', but in reality there could be if you don't see yourself reflected in the things around you."

We would like her to present to us a single black person who was negatively impacted by writing on white paper.

Ever.

We use our brains when discussing political policy, rather than automatically connecting said policy to the color of someone's skin. And when we Chicks get attacked on our website or Facebook page with the accusation of "RACIST!" we typically ask our attacker to have a seat with us, stay awhile, and debate an actual issue. And predictably, that usually runs them right off.

And it's not just random folks on Facebook making the racism accusation, but leaders of institutions that are built specifically to examine "race and justice." Like Charles Ogletree, founder and executive director of the Charles Hamilton Houston Institute for Race and Justice.

CHARLES OGLETREE AND "UPPITY PROFESSORS"

In early 2010, Charles Ogletree accused Sarah Palin of being racist, because at a Tea Party convention, Palin said, "They know we're at war, and to win that war we need a commander in chief, not a professor of law standing at the lectern."[2]

If you're a person with an *actual brain*, you're reading that quote and thinking, "Where in the holy hell is there anything remotely racist in that statement?" Well, Ogletree (founder and executive director of the Charles Hamilton Houston Institute for Race and Justice) explained that he believes the "professor" label is a "thinly veiled attack on Obama's race." Why? Because it's nearly synonymous with calling Obama "uppity," which is a term Ogletree also believes carries racial overtones.

If you're shaking your head in bewilderment right now, congratulations. You are a normal human being.

Ogletree explained more about the professor label:

> *The idea is that he's not one of us. He has these ideas that are left wing, that are socialist, that he's palling around with terrorists—those were buzzwords, but the reality was they*

were looking at this president as an African American who was out of place.

This is how pathetic the liberals' favorite accusation has become. It's racist to call Obama a professor, because it implies he's being looked at as a black person who's out of his element.

Which begs the question, as the *Wall Street Journal* asked, isn't it, then, even worse to refer to him as president?

Ogletree's assertion that the word "professor" was racist was moronic but sadly indicative of how absurd the racism accusation has become. Now, not only do we need to be mindful of the inherent racism in common, everyday words like "professor," but we need to feel guilty about our whiteness, too.

WHITE PRIVILEGE IN MINNESOTA

If it weren't already bad enough that we are faced with endless racism accusations, some liberals are even taking it a step further, and demanding that white people feel extra guilt for being white.

Case in point. Let's look at the University of Minnesota.

We could have almost forgiven Minnesota for Jesse Ventura. But then they went and elected Al Franken as a U.S. senator. And if that weren't enough, they went completely off the deep end and decided that aspiring teachers need "cultural competence testing."[3]

Apparently, the University of Minnesota thinks that the reason their minority students aren't doing well academically is because the teachers lack *cultural competence.* To fix this problem, the university created a Race, Culture, Class, and Gender Task Group. The task group's resulting report suggests that race, class, and gender politics should be the "overarching framework" for all those teaching classes at the university.[4] We're not making this up. A solid academic foundation? Nah. Who needs that? What we need is a solid race/class/gender politics framework. Yeah. That'll fix everything.

How do prospective teachers acquire cultural competence, you might ask? Well, according to the report, the first thing they have to do is look deep within themselves to identify and then admit their own prejudices. They should question their own motives for wanting to teach, and also take a special "cultural intelligence assessment."

All that ancillary nonsense—like arithmetic and reading and spelling—isn't really important. It's cultural intelligence that will help minority students do better on, say, a biology test.

In the task group's own words, they want to ensure that "future teachers will be able to discuss their own histories and current thinking drawing on notions of white privilege. . . . Future teachers must also recognize and denounce the fundamental injustices at the heart of American society, [and] explain how institutional racism works in schools."[5]

Can you even believe this crap? They may as well just gather all of the minority kids in a room and tell them that America sucks, and that they have absolutely no prayer for achieving anything, and that working hard is useless, because that's pretty much the message here. And if you think that task group is bad, wait'll you hear about the White Privilege Conference that is held annually.

Even though Minnesota's Lakeville public schools saw cuts in teacher staff, their arts program, and the closing of a whole school as a result of their $7 million budget cut, they did have plenty of Minnesota taxpayer money to send several of their teachers to the White Privilege Conference held in Minneapolis (and to pay substitute teachers in their absence). The conference attendees got to participate in workshops on "how

PEANUT BUTTER SANDWICHES ARE RACIST

It actually physically hurt our brains to read about a Portland, Oregon, principal named Verenice Gutierrez who "picks up on the subtle language of racism" on a daily basis.

She said, "Take the peanut butter sandwich, a seemingly innocent example a teacher used in a lesson last school year. What about Somali or Hispanic students, who might not eat sandwiches? Another way would be to say: 'Americans eat peanut butter and jelly, do you have anything like that?' Let them tell you. Maybe they eat torta. Or pita."[6]

While this principal in Oregon wastes time worrying about pita and torta being discriminated against, kids in European and Asian countries are being taught actual math and science skills. They're going to be developing nuclear-powered portals to different dimensions or something, while our kids are taught to recognize their own white privilege in the form of PB&J.

Awesome.

white privilege, white supremacy, and oppression affect daily life."[7] Because don't you see how all of this is *totally relevant* to education? Don't you see how all of these white-guilt workshops will help kids? Don't you, you white privileged jerks?

Seriously. Enough with this politically correct, white privilege, racial-overtones-in-everything crap. You know what would really help make society more colorblind? If we stopped talking about race all the time and focused instead on peoples' character.

And that's what conservatives are right to do. Whether you're a person of color or a person of pallor, conservatives judge you by your character.

Unfortunately, black Americans have aligned themselves with Democrats for decades, which has been wildly successful for Democrats. But can black Americans really say the same? Has the Democratic Party served them well? (Hint: the answer is no.)

DEMOCRATS HAVEN'T HELPED BLACK PEOPLE

Let's be real here. Democrat policies have hurt black Americans for decades. But don't take it from two lily-white chicks. Take it from Walter Williams, a black American economist at George Mason University, who said it best when he explained, "The welfare state has done to black Americans what slavery could not have done, namely break up the black family."[8] He went on to say that just over 30 percent of black children live in two-parent families, compared to 75–90 percent until the 1940s. This is a direct result of welfare policies, because as Williams points out, "If you subsidize anything, you're going to get surpluses of it, and if you tax something, you're going to get less of it." What would happen if there was no welfare? People would have to decide to live more responsibly. Government, through the implementation of liberal welfare programs, Williams said, has made black male fathers dispensable.

Or take it from Thomas Sowell, a black American senior fellow at the Hoover Institution, who wrote that Democrat-imposed minimum wage policies have directly and negatively impacted black people.[9] When Roosevelt established minimum wages in 1933, for example, blacks lost a half million jobs. There is indisputable evidence that continuously raising the minimum wage creates high unemployment, especially among minorities. And what happens when there's high unemployment among minorities? Too many are recruited into lives of crime, and too many are enticed onto the government dole. Too many blacks were lured by Democrats into homes they couldn't really afford when Democrats went on an "affordable housing crusade" and high rates of subsequent foreclosures ended up reducing the number of black-owned homes to levels *lower* than before the crusade began.

Or take it from David A. Clarke Jr., the sheriff of Milwaukee County, Wisconsin (and a black American), who wrote an op-ed in the *Washington Times* in which he suggested, "White liberal social policies have become the new racism in America."[10]

One of our favorite conservative converts, State Senator Elbert Guillory of Louisiana, left the Democratic Party because he recognized that programs like welfare, food stamps, and other entitlements aren't designed to lift black Americans out of poverty, but rather, they were "always intended as a mechanism for politicians to control the black community."[11]

We quite agree with him. And with Williams. And with Sowell. And with Clarke. And these are just a few examples.

If you still don't believe us that liberal policies have hurt black Americans, then consider that the out-of-wedlock birthrate among African Americans today has tripled since the War on Poverty. And according to David Horowitz and John Perazzo's booklet *Government Versus the People*, the kids raised in homes without dads are "far more likely to grow up poor and to eventually engage in criminal behavior than their peers who are raised in two-parent homes."[12] The Census Bureau reported that in 2010 the black poverty rate was 27.4 percent (about three times higher than for whites), meaning that 11.5 million blacks in the United States were living in poverty.[13]

That doesn't sound very "progressive" now, does it?

Democrats capitalize on black suffering by telling black Americans that their policies will help them. As a result, Democrats typically get around 90 percent of the black vote, and the cycle is perpetuated.[14] Liberals pander away, using black folks as pawns in the political game, insisting that Republicans are racist and hate black people (and the poor, and the working class, and anyone who doesn't look like them, etc.). We'll hand it to them—Democrats are calculating and politically savvy. They know that blacks are turning out in higher numbers than whites to vote in elections these days, and they will do whatever it takes—other than actually helping them—to keep those votes.[15]

Think about the messaging that Democrats use in every single campaign. "We want to help you," they say. "We want to take care of you. We stand up for the poor and underprivileged!" And then they create entitlement programs disguised as "help" when in reality, those programs simply enslave. During Obama's time in office, welfare-program spending jumped 32 percent,[16] but joblessness and the labor force participation rate dropped to a level seen only during the stagflation of the 1970s.[17] The Great Unifier hasn't helped black people (or white people, for that matter). In fact, he and his Democrat friends have assumed the worst about black people, and as a result they've *created* an environment that breeds failure. Republicans have a hard sell here. Democrats get to say, "We will *give* you stuff!" while Republicans are saying, "We want you to *earn* stuff!" If you were an unemployed salesperson looking for a high-commission sales job, whose message would you rather peddle?

It's easy to grab freebies. Conservatives don't blame people for wanting to get ahead—we want more for people, because we believe in the American dream for anyone who wants to pursue it. Part of that dream, though, is freedom from the enslavement of the government. Unfortunately, the party favored by black Americans is the same party that breeds dependence on government. It's what that party is all about.

And that's why conservatives are right.

Racism exists. We know that. But while Democrats are busy

screaming "Racism!" from the rooftops, the pulpits, the news desks, and any and every other place they can to perpetuate the idea that we're a nation of skin-color-obsessed jackwagons, conservatives are busy thinking about important things like the content of people's character or their ability to get a job done.

If people would do *less* talking about race, we'd be much better off in this country. But alas, it's something we are forced to discuss. So conservatives need to get in there and start talking about it, openly, and with clarity. We need to directly address every race and nationality and help them understand exactly what self-sufficiency means. We can lift them up. We can give them the best handout of all—a hand up. We can give them the best gift of all—the American dream.

CHAPTER 8

The War on Women Is Crap

Oh, the War on Women. Liberals are so obsessed with their manufactured woman war that they crafted the entire last presidential campaign around it—successfully, unfortunately. You could barely get through a single newspaper or TV show during the 2012 election cycle without hearing about the Republican War on Women ad nauseum. From the Internet to the evening news to our sitcoms and movies, you name it—everyone was talking about the Republican War on Women. Because those Republican meanies are *so mean!*

Obama won a second term because liberal women lapped up the War on Women narrative like Nancy Pelosi at an all-you-can-inject Botox buffet. They believed everything they were told and did everything the Democrats told them to do, performing as model political pawns. And then they called themselves empowered and progressive and *feminist*. For real.

Conservatives are right to be pissed off at the narrative that the Democrats tell, because it's the biggest boldfaced lie since the invention of Prince Charming. Leftist feminists have hijacked feminism, and in the process have made a mockery of everything women have worked their asses off to achieve to date. Their way of thinking is completely counter to the notion of empowerment—or feminism. Their hysteria is so misdirected, their anger so misplaced, and their inner turmoil so misguided—it makes us want to scoop them up and put them into our pockets, because it's clear that they have absolutely no business wandering around the country without direct supervision. These chicks have set us *back* about fifty freaking years with the crap they're peddling these days.

Unfortunately, they have an arsenal of media elite on their side. You see, Democrats are in the unpleasant position of being on the defensive in the wake of this administration's failed economic policies. But they know what formula works for them—the tried-and-true tactic of social fear mongering. And weak women eat this crap up.

Conservatives are right to push back on the Left's hypocrisy in its treatment of women. We're right to scoff at the claims that Republicans are trying to deny women access to birth control. We're absolutely right to call politicians out when they try to convince their followers that Republicans have the power to take away their access to abortions. And conservatives are spot-on when we turn the War on Women back on the real perpetrators of it—liberals themselves.

However, we're also right to call out our own when we see fellow conservatives exemplifying behaviors that damage our cause. We're equal-opportunity criticizers, as it happens.

But let's start with the most obvious liberal hypocrisy in this War on Women. Because even as liberals convince their followers of how horrible and mean conservatives are to women, they trot out messengers who are positively misogynistic. When liberal messengers are dreadful to *conservative* women, no one flinches.

WHO'S CALLING NAMES?

We find it condescendingly one-sided when liberals freak out at Rush Limbaugh's now-famous "slut" statement about Sandra

Fluke (liberal chicks love playing victim to Limbaugh), yet conveniently ignore Bill Maher's calling conservative women "bimbos" and "c*nts." They couldn't care less that so-called journalist Ed Schultz referred to Laura Ingraham as a "slut." And what liberal ever brings up that whole statutory-rape joke David Letterman made about Sarah Palin's daughter? Men who call women sluts, c*nts, or bimbos are both objectifying and degrading women. That includes liberal men. But we have learned that in the eyes of liberal "feminists," condescending, degrading words are only offensive when the woman being called those names is a fellow liberal. If it's a conservative woman being called derogatory names? It's called comedy, you sticks in the mud. Get with the program.

Again with that whole setting-us-back-fifty-years thing.

THE WAR ON BIRTH CONTROL?

One common claim liberals like to use in their War on Women fairy tale is that Republicans, because they expect people to have financial responsibility for their own sex lives (*the horror!*), have made it more difficult to get birth control, an argument Shushannah Walshe made in *Marie Claire* magazine.[1] Erin Gloria Ryan on *Jezebel* went further, claiming, "If birth control is less accessible, then less women will be on birth control."[2] The problem with those statements (other than Ryan's unfortunate grammar) is that there isn't a speck of data that shows Republicans have made it more difficult for a woman to get birth control in this free market country. As conservative women who have taken birth control pills on and off for over four collective decades, we know that access is not—and has never been—an issue. Birth control pills are available on the Internet, or we can ask our partner to buy some condoms, or if that's not easy enough, we can visit our local Walmart and purchase birth control for around nine dollars. And listen, we're not anyone's financial planner and we're the first ones to admit our deep-seated hatred of math, but it seems to us that if a woman can't afford nine-dollar birth control pills each month, her iPhone just became less important to hold on to, let alone her subscription to or monthly purchase of *Marie Claire* magazine. That's just called common sense.

What liberal feminists can't seem to fathom is that real women in the real world have bigger concerns than having Joe Q. Taxpayer pay for their little packs of pills.

To be clear, no one is suggesting that women not have access to birth control. In fact, we Chicks are huge fans of people responsibly managing their own reproductive activities (and we're especially huge fans of the idea of *liberal* women using birth control—*liberally*). If Walshe or Ryan could cite where any conservative suggests banning condoms from the entire marketplace, for example, that'd be great. The claim that fewer women will be on birth control if birth control is less accessible is, translated from Liberal to English, "If birth control isn't free for women like me, then we will be irresponsible idiots who get pregnant because we don't want to have to buy our own birth control. And that means gobs and gobs and gobs of unplanned babies, because conservatives won't let us get abortions." That's their argument, you guys. We just put it in words that accurately describe their position. They should try that sometime.

The thing that disturbs us most about the War on Women narrative is the fact that it ties feminism to reproductive rights.

LIBERAL CHICKS' OBSESSION WITH LADYPARTS

In 2013, the University of Sydney student newspaper *Honi Soit* was yanked by the Student Representative Council because the cover featured the photographs of eighteen different women's vulvas.[3] The magazine said they wanted to show vaginas/vulvas in a nonsexual way, as an exercise in "female empowerment."[4] When the SRC deemed it inappropriate for the newsstands, *Honi Soit* was outraged, and said, "That in 2013, vulvas can still be considered something that should be shunned and hidden, or offensive, is absurd."

They believed that vulvas needed "liberating," and were totally perplexed as to why reasonable people might not want to see eighteen photos of women's vulvas on their newsstands. Because after all, as they pointed out, "What is offensive or obscene about a body part that over half of the Australian population have? Why can't we talk about it—why can't we see it?"

And then they got downright defiant. They wrote, "By distributing this cover about the university, we have given our audience no choice. Either accept vaginas as normal, non-threatening, and not disgusting, or explain why you can't."

Here's the thing, you *Honi Soit* ladypart-obsessed weirdos. We happily accept our vaginas as normal and nonthreatening and not disgusting, but we *also* choose to not display them to anyone and everyone. We know this is shocking, but it's possible to view female reproductive organs as beautiful and natural and lovely and *private* all at the same time. There is nothing wrong with a little modesty. Modesty is not the same as shame and it's not the same as embarrassment and it's not the same as disgust. Just because over half of the population has a particular body part doesn't mean we need to view eighteen images of said body part on the cover of a paper. Vaginas and vulvas exist. Women have them. They come in all sorts of shapes and sizes and colors. They are regular, normal parts of a female body. But they are also sexual organs, and there is nothing wrong with a culture treating sex and its related parts as a private, personal thing. There is nothing wrong with a culture that appreciates a little mystery as it relates to intimacy.

What liberal feminists can't seem to fathom is that real women in the real world have bigger concerns than having Joe Q. Taxpayer pay for their little packs of pills. We care about things like those jobs we're losing, out-of-control gas prices, ridiculous spikes in our grocery bills, and every day utility prices skyrocketing. We care about whether or not we'll be able to put food on our families' tables. We care about the fact that under Obama's administration, millions more women live in poverty because of his sucky policies—by September 2011, for example, 800,000 more women were in poverty than when Obama took office,[5] and 780,000 women had lost their jobs.[6] We care about making sure our children aren't going to be burdened with debt that will inevitably bankrupt this country. We care about things like personal responsibility—both fiscal and reproductive. Isn't it more empowering to be a woman who manages her own reproductive system than to be a woman who relies on others to manage and pay for it on her behalf? That's the truth about most Republican women—we don't assume other women are incapable of taking care of their own birth control the way Democrats do. We assume the opposite, because if you think about it, it's downright demeaning to women to assume that they're not equipped to handle their own birth control. Conservative women like us Chicks believe in the strength and fortitude of women. We don't expect a handout. We don't expect special treatment, because we're strong enough to take care of ourselves. We don't believe in government acting as a sugar daddy, which is exactly what liberal "feminists" seem to insist on, at the expense of other hardworking taxpayers. Liberal feminists demand that the government stay out of their bedroom, but apparently have no problem demanding that taxpayers fork over their hard-earned money to fund what they do in there.

It's not a war on birth control to believe that religious organizations that vehemently oppose both contraception and abortive measures should not be forced to provide those services to their employees. Religious freedom far transcends the desire of women who simply want free birth control. No one is required to work for a specific employer. No one is required to stay with an employer whose health plan isn't acceptable to them. People have choices. There's this thing called the free market, whereby if enough people get pissed off at an employer for not providing something in their health plan, the employer may be inclined to provide that something after all, simply to ensure that it can recruit and keep quality employees.

This isn't about access to contraception—it's about *personal responsibility*. The minute that women give up that notion and depend on others to provide for them is the minute that real feminism dies.

But the War on Women campaign isn't just about contraception. Liberals would be lost if they couldn't use abortion as the main pillar in their claim that Republicans are staging a woman war.

ABORTION = LIBERAL BIRTH CONTROL

We mentioned the *Jezebel* article that suggested there's some sort of push to prevent women from accessing birth control. What we should also point out is that to many liberals, abortion *is* birth control. And when they get themselves all wound up about the possibility of *Roe v. Wade* being overturned, and abortion being outlawed, they sound like crazy people.

Most conservatives would love to see the Supreme Court overturn *Roe v. Wade* and leave decisions about abortion laws to individual states. But liberals often make it sound as though elected conservatives have some sort of magic wand that they could simply wave once sworn in, to actually make that happen. Let's suppose we all live in that fantasyland for a moment. Here are the things that would have to *actually happen* for their worst nightmare to become reality.

A conservative president would have to win election and *then*

1. Have an opportunity to replace a liberal justice; and then
2. Senators would have to confirm that justice; and then
3. That justice would have to be supportive of overturning *Roe v. Wade*; and then
4. That justice would have to create a majority on the court willing to revisit *Roe v. Wade*; and then
5. There would have to be an appropriate case for the court to review; and then
6. The court would have to rule to fully overturn *Roe v. Wade*, returning abortion regulations to the states.

Then, and *only* then, could a state legislature vote to end safe, legal abortion. Seriously, you might as well add "if purple unicorns invade Congress" to the list of things that would have to happen for these concerns to actually come to fruition.

It's pretty much a nonissue, folks.

More disturbing than the false panic about the overturn of *Roe v. Wade* is the liberal idea that abortion is a normal form of birth control. Take the assertion in that same *Jezebel* article that electing a conservative president would be the "end of dating as we know it" because "having sex in a world without safe, available abortion is like penis Russian roulette."[7] Translation: abortion *is* contraception, like we said. And that, clever and competent readers, is *wack*. You would think that these women had never heard of condoms.

In the very same column, the argument was made that "Reducing access to birth control and abortion has never, not once, in all of human history resulted in people foregoing recreational sex." Wait. Didn't they just complain that reducing access to birth control and abortion would end dating as we know it? And now they say that people's sex lives wouldn't change? Make up your minds, liberal feminists.

We know our clever and competent readers are able to cut through this kind of crap without the help of a single ginsu knife. But it's important to point out that an entire presidential campaign was centered around this War on Women, we-think-only-with-our-ladyparts *crap*. And it worked. And it continues to work, much to our dismay.

Just think, in another part of the world, a young woman named Malala Yousafzai was shot in the face at point-blank range by the Taliban because she's female and wanted to be educated. After surviving that shooting, she spends her time spreading her message of true female empowerment. Malala isn't complaining about the cost of birth control, and she's not demanding carefree and convenient abortion services. She's advocating for things that really matter to girls and women, like equal education opportunities for females, regardless of their social, economic, legal, or political standing. She's pushing for the rights of girls and women everywhere to have a voice and to be fearless in their pursuit of knowledge and learning. Liberal feminists could take a lesson from her about what a War on Women really looks like.

And they could also take a look at their own Democratic Party campaign strategy to see just how synonymous the Democratic Party is with an *actual* War on Women. They needn't look further than that Democrat-invented female parasite named Julia. You remember Julia, don't you?

THE LAMENTABLE LIFE OF POOR, DEPENDENT, FUTURE-LIBERAL-FEMINIST JULIA

One of the more remarkable marketing ploys that the Obama administration used to woo voters during the 2012 election was the "Life of Julia" slideshow posted on the official Obama website. (The entire slideshow has since been removed from the website, although the placeholder still exists,[8] as do countless references and screengrabs all over the Internet.[9]) The slideshow attempted to demonstrate what a complete slice of awesome it would be if Obama were to be reelected. Life for Julia under Obama was a cradle-to-grave, nanny-state utopia.

For example, the slide for Julia at age three read:

Julia is enrolled in a Head Start program to help get her ready for school. Because of steps President Obama has taken to improve programs like this one, Julia joins thousands of students across the country who will start kindergarten ready to learn and succeed.

The slide for Julia at age eighteen read:

Julia and her family qualify for President Obama's American Opportunity Tax Credit—worth up to $10,000 over four years. Julia is also one of millions of students who receive a Pell Grant to help put a college education within reach.

The slide for Julia at age twenty-two read:

During college, Julia undergoes surgery. It is thankfully covered by her insurance due to a provision in health care reform that lets her stay on her parents' coverage until she turns 26.

The slide for Julia at age thirty-one read:

Julia decides to have a child. Throughout her pregnancy, she benefits from maternal checkups, prenatal care, and free screenings under health care reform.

And that was just the beginning. Julia's entire life was mapped out on Obama's website, and from start to finish, it focused on all of the government programs Julia could rely on under President Obama. It focused on what could be done *for* her, through taxpayer money, rather than what she could do for *herself* as an empowered, capable female. What that handy-dandy slideshow neglected to do was give Julia a shred of credit for having a brain of her own. Julia was made out to be a helpless, dependent parasite. The ad creators might as well have told women not to worry their pretty little heads about grown-up matters.

Like we said earlier, liberal feminists lapped it up. Never mind that a recently concluded study showed that "by third grade, the $8 billion Head Start program had little to no impact on cognitive, social-emotional, health, or parenting practices of participants. On a few measures, access to Head Start had harmful effects on children."[10] Never mind that the Pell Grant program is just another entitlement funded by taxpayers, with a predictable record of abuse.[11]

And never mind that the government programs mentioned in that pathetic "Life of Julia" slideshow are, by and large, epic failures. Never mind that they are unsustainable and likely won't be available to Julia, or anyone else for that matter, within the next few decades.

Never mind *reality.* Liberals don't want to hear about facts and figures. They don't want to acknowledge that "free" actually isn't free at all. They'd rather rely on emotional blackmail to advance their agenda, and they'd rather sell a false narrative that only perpetuates the notion that women can't handle themselves responsibly enough to make it through life without someone else's assistance—in this case, government's.

Conservatives know better.

So while you might be (correctly) thinking, "Why doesn't Julia freaking grow a pair already and pay for her own crap?" liberals look at that slideshow and respond with applause. Because they are *all about* cradle-to-grave government. Dependency is their calling card.

And these fools accuse *Republicans* of setting women back?! Seriously?

But here's what's really interesting. Liberal feminists built their entire movement around *independence* from men, and shunned the *Mad Men*–era "sugar daddy" as being oppressive. They snubbed their noses at women who married for financial security. And then somewhere along the way, even as they proudly proclaimed how strong and independent they were, liberal feminists hilariously decided that even though they didn't need sugar daddy *men* to take care of them, they *did* need sugar daddy *taxpayers* to. So it's no wonder they looked to Obama as their knight in shining armor, there to whisk them away from the financial and logistical realities of mean ol' life.

Liberal feminists are quick to mock women who *choose* a traditional stay-at-home-wife/mother role as their profession and allow their husbands to support them. Think back to Hillary Clinton's famous quote during her husband's first presidential campaign: "I suppose I could have stayed home and baked cookies and had teas, but what I decided to do was to fulfill my profession, which I entered before my husband was in public life." That was Hillary's way of minimizing women who were supported financially by their husbands. Apparently, liberal feminists find women who are supported by their husbands to be worthy of scorn. *But they have no issue whatsoever with women being dependent on the government.*

So our question is: What's the damn difference? Why is it so distasteful to liberal feminists for a woman to rely on a husband for her financial security, but completely acceptable to demand that the government pay for contraception? Think about it. It's really just two different varieties of dependency: one comes with a wedding ring, and the other comes with a NuvaRing.

. . . .

Regardless of whether you're depending on a man to take care of you or millions of taxpayers to take care of you, you're *still* relying on a sugar daddy.

. . . .

Listen, we are not knocking women (as Hillary Clinton did) who choose the traditional stay-at-home role. It's a respectable choice, particularly when staying at home means raising a family. Raising a family is hard work—we Chicks know that firsthand—and we have mad respect for men who recognize that and make it financially possible for their wives to pursue that nonsalaried, chosen career full-time. There's an honest partnership that happens in that type of household.

Moreover, one of the pillars of real feminism is *choice,* right? So why begrudge a woman for making her own vocational choices in life? If that choice is to stay at home and raise children and run a household with a willing husband who supports that choice, then why exactly is that a bad thing?

We think it's time for liberals to at least be honest about this. Regardless of whether you're depending on a man to take care of you or millions of taxpayers to take care of you, you're *still relying on a sugar daddy.* And consider this. If a sugar daddy man willingly enters a relationship with a woman with the intention of providing for her financially (either partially or wholly), that is *voluntary.* That's not the case when a sugar daddy is wrapped up in a government package with a pretty bow on top paid for by John and Jane Q. Taxpayer. When the sugar daddy is the government (read: taxpayers), that financial support is taken *involuntarily.* And if you ask us, that's a hell of a lot more contemptible.

When liberals demand taxpayers foot the bill for their choices, they are the *worst kind* of dependent. They are the antithesis of everything they claim they want to be. They demand benevolence and charity at gunpoint. They aren't independent. They're bratty kids who think the world owes them something. They're parasites.

They're Julia.

The government has become the liberals' collective sugar daddy. And Barack Obama is their daddy in chief, ready to

BIRTH CONTROL VS. VIAGRA

Liberals who don't understand human physiology often like to argue that contraception should be a covered benefit under insurance plans because Viagra is often covered for men. Let's just clear this up once and for all.

First of all, insurance plans vary from company to company, employer to employer, state to state, and premium rate to premium rate. Some cover Viagra, some don't. But here's why that's completely irrelevant. Viagra is used to treat a medical problem. It is used to fix something that is not working the way it's supposed to.

Erectile dysfunction is a medical condition whereby a penis *does not function properly*. Medications used to treat this condition allow a nonworking penis to do what it is *naturally supposed to do*.

Female contraception is a way of *preventing* a perfectly working set of reproductive organs from working the way they are *naturally supposed to*.

We are so sick of people using the "Why should insurance cover Viagra and not birth control pills?" argument. When used for birth control, female contraceptive pills prevent a female body from becoming pregnant. In other words, *there is no medical problem they are fixing when their purpose is for birth control*.

We fail to see why this is so complicated for some people to understand. No one is suggesting that birth control pills be withheld from a woman when they are prescribed to treat an actual medical problem. So before anyone screams, "But I use birth control for polycystic ovarian syndrome!" or whatever other medical condition you might have that birth control is used for, *no one is saying* that you shouldn't be covered for that. What we are saying is that if you are simply using birth control pills to not get pregnant, why should we subsidize that? When we have a monthly massage, it prevents the neck strain we tend to get from working on our computers every day. Pony up, liberals. *We need* the massages, and they are *preventive*.

Maybe taxpayers should foot the bill for everyone to have as much to eat as they want, as much medical care for free as they want, as big of a house as they want, free cell phones, free cars, etc., etc., etc. Because people need that stuff, you guys. Who cares how it'll all get paid for? Let's just let the next generations worry about that while we run around getting all of our "needs" met.

Free abortions for everyone! Whoo hooooooooo!

We're just waiting for liberal chicks to start demanding taxpayers foot the bill for their feminine-hygiene products next. And this is why we mock them. It's why we mock the entire War on Women—because it's one of the greatest tricks ever played on the American people by one of the most manipulative administrations in history. And sadly, it worked.

save them from all the perils of individualism, competence, and strength that our foremothers fought for back in the day.

Put simply, there is no War on Women, other than the one that the Left has created as a political campaign strategy. If you want birth control, *buy it*. If you work for a religious organization that opposes birth control or abortion, either find a new employer or shut up already.

Conservatives are right to believe in the collective strength and ability of women to take care of themselves. We're right to refrain from insulting the intelligence of women by suggesting that they simply couldn't make it through life without government holding their hands through every milestone. And we're right to set high standards for ourselves and other women when it comes to demonstrating our independence and intellectual horsepower.

Which is why it's so frustrating when we discover that other conservatives are contributing to the problem. Like the Tone-Deaf Todds, for example.

THE TONE-DEAF TODDS: WHEN REPUBLICANS SHOOT THEMSELVES IN THE FOOT

In our quest to make over conservatism, nothing frustrates us more than when fellow conservatives exemplify the very stereotypes from which we are trying to distance ourselves. We should and must call out misogynistic behaviors, as we did in the fall of 2013 with Indiana representative Todd Rokita, who concluded a debate about the 2013 government shutdown and Obamacare with Carol Costello, a CNN host, by telling her she was "beautiful" but that she needed to be "honest." That wasn't a compliment—it was condescension. Representative Rokita did exactly nothing to shatter the stereotype of Republicans being a bunch of misogynistic white dudes when he, a white Republican dude, couldn't manage to make points about policy and ideology without resorting to commenting on Carol Costello's appearance. So yes, of course we need to identify cases of blatant sexism and say, "Hey—that is *not cool*, sexist person. And you need to stop that."

Shortly after the Rokita video became the laughing stock of many liberal websites, we decided to talk on our radio show about how disappointed we were that he had made Carol Costello's appearance a part of the conversation at all.

Because you know what? We agreed with absolutely every last one of Todd Rokita's policy points. He spoke eloquently on the government shutdown of 2013 and on Obamacare. He used strong arguments that would have held up well on their own. The moment he brought Costello's appearance into the equation, though, his arguments were completely diluted. We know that if the reporter had been a super hot dude, Rokita would not have said, "Look, you're a really handsome fellow, but you need to be honest." Of course he wouldn't have. *And that is why it was a problem*. We knew that, and we pointed it out.

· ·

We know that if the reporter had been a superhot dude, Rokita would not have said, "Look, you're a really handsome fellow, but you need to be honest." Of course he wouldn't have. *And that is why it was a problem.*

· ·

That made a lot of our fellow conservatives mad. They called us. And wrote us. And after we spoke about this on our radio show, they said we were making a mountain out of a molehill and that we should support and defend Rokita on this. They told us that we "shouldn't eat our own." And you know what? Had his spat with Carol Costello stayed strictly about the issues, we *would've* defended him. On policy matters, which is what the conversation should have been about, we agreed with him entirely. But what we *couldn't* defend, regardless of whether we shared his political affiliation, was the condescending and sexist way he chose to respond to her. Not cool.

Conservatives are right to push back against the misogynistic stereotype that is often associated with us, which is why we're not about to let conservatives off the hook when they do stupid crap. We're about giving conservatism a makeover. And if that means we have to call out conservatives for bad behavior sometimes, we're going to do just that.

We were anxious to talk with Congressman Rokita personally about his exchange with Carol Costello, and invited him on our show. He declined. He also released this statement:

> *At the end of a spirited and very important debate, I was simply keeping it from unnecessarily ending in an unfriendly or contentious way. I intended no offense to Ms. Costello.*

Is that the lamest statement ever, or what? Rokita should have simply said, "You know what? That was a boneheaded move on my part, and I'm sorry I brought her appearance into the conversation at all. My bad." And that would've been fine. Saying you "intended no offense" isn't apologizing for your own behavior; it's suggesting that if someone was offended by your behavior, that's their problem.

Not cool.

Unfortunately, Rokita wasn't the only Tone-Deaf Todd of 2013. Enter the original: Todd Akin.

Sigh.

In August 2012, Republican Todd Akin was gearing up to unseat Democrat Senator Claire McCaskill in Missouri and actually had a sizeable lead against her in the polls, when he decided to make the following comment during a TV interview: "First of all, from what I understand from doctors [pregnancy from rape is] really rare. If it's a legitimate rape, the female body has ways to try to shut that whole thing down."[12]

It came as no surprise to us or to any other reasonable conservative when Akin's campaign came to a screeching halt

right after that. "Legitimate rape"? And women's bodies having mechanisms of "shutting that whole thing down"?

Oy vey.

And if that weren't enough, a couple months later Akin
likened Claire McCaskill to a dog playing fetch and then fol-
lowed that up with a comment that McCaskill was far more
"ladylike" a few years prior.[13]

It's as if he had a Democratic strategist working for him on
the sly, telling him precisely what to do to make Republicans
look as bad as they could possibly look.

Democrats delighted in pointing at Akin and saying, "See?
That's how Republicans are." Akin became the de facto face of
Republicans, and it was a pimply, wart-covered, hideous face.

We know better, and so do most conservatives. Todd Akin
is not the face of Republicans. The real faces of conservatism
are you and me. The problem is that low-information voters
don't know this, so we lose elections.

The Tone-Deaf Todds are part of the reason we talk about
conservatism needing a makeover. They make the scam that is
the War on Women look real and distract people from the real
issues at hand. We're spending way too much time explaining
that, no, conservatives aren't all misogynists when we could be
fighting more important battles. Plus, we've got our own wars to
contend with happening on our website and Facebook page every single day.

WAR ON THE CHICKS!

You want to see what a real War on Women looks like? Take a
gander at messages we received on our social media platforms
within just one month.

From Michael on Facebook:

> You guys are perfect to fill vacant time. Matches your vacant morals. Did you ask your man if it's ok for you to work outside the home? Don't forget your burka when you go out. You know those boys will just rape you.

From Bart on Facebook:

> Nothing but a bunch of elitist C*NTS!

From T.A.:

> Change the name of this page to Murdoch bimbo chics on the wrong.

Yeah. This is a day in the life of the Chicks. We're women who simply run a website, have a radio show, and are active on social media so that we can express ourselves freely and reach out to like-minded conservatives. And these are the kinds of attacks we face in response.

But there's a *Republican War on Women*, everyone!

CHAPTER 9

We Are Pro-Life

Remember back in the Clinton years when the goal was to make abortions "safe, legal, and rare"? Something has changed over the last few decades. Somehow, all stealth-like, the Democrat goal seems to have become making abortions "easy, accessible, and convenient." You know, just like fast food. Or Starbucks. If it were up to the most rabid pro-choicers, abortion clinics would be open on every street corner, preferably with drive-through service. Or they'd be *in* Starbucks. Because wouldn't that be so super handy? And *empowering*?

Conservatives are right to be pro-life. We are right to defend the rights of the weakest humans. After all, what more important thing is there to fight for than *life itself*? For the rights of future generations to exist? We understand that's legal for women to have abortions but we are right to insist that they know exactly what they are doing when they have them.

THERE'S PRO-LIFE OR PRO-ABORTION. THAT'S THE CHOICE.

While sparring in the third debate of the 2008 presidential campaign, then senator Obama talked about his own stance on abortion:

> *Surely there is some common ground when both those who believe in choice and those who are opposed to abortion can come together. . . . We should try to prevent unintended pregnancies by providing appropriate education to our youth, communicating that sexuality is sacred and that they should not be engaged in cavalier activity, and providing options for adoption, and helping single mothers if they want to choose to keep the baby. . . . Nobody's pro-abortion. I think it's always a tragic situation. We should try to reduce these circumstances.*[1]

We're huge proponents of that whole education thing the POTUS speaks of there. We also love communication, *when it's truthful*. So here's some truth for you. Although Obama has stated his "aversion to partial birth abortion," his voting record suggests otherwise.[2] It's weird how the prez didn't share *that* little tidbit in his little speech, isn't it? Leftist politicians have a habit of not sharing unsavory records, for some odd reason. Instead, they gravitate toward words like "choice" and "situation" and "circumstances," which sound a whole hell of a lot better to a crowd of low-information voters who don't really want to hear about jamming scissors into a baby's skull and sucking his brains out and whatnot.

Let's be real. There's really no such thing as "pro-choice" in the abortion debate. There's either pro-life or pro-abortion. Period. Renaming abortion to more palatable terms like "reproductive choice" or "bodily autonomy" or whatever other distracting verbiage the liberal public relations machine generates doesn't change what abortions are. And if you still have doubts, we recommend you do some reading beyond this book. We suggest testimonials from people who have performed actual abortions, like Dr. Anthony Levatino, who testified in front of a congressional committee back in May 2013 about the 1,200-plus abortions he performed. Some of those abortions were babies twenty weeks or older, and his testimony was decidedly clinical:

> *The toughest part of a D&E abortion is extracting the baby's head. The head of a baby that age is about the size of a large plum and is now free floating inside the uterine cavity. You can be pretty sure you have hold of it if the Sopher clamp is spread about as far as your fingers will allow. You will know you have it right when you crush down on the clamp and see white gelatinous material coming through the cervix. That was the baby's brains. You can then extract the skull pieces. Many times a little face will come out and stare back at you.*
>
> *Congratulations! You have just successfully performed a second-trimester suction D&E abortion. You just affirmed her right to choose.*
>
> *If you refuse to believe that this procedure inflicts severe pain on that unborn child, please think again.*

That's the reality of being "pro-choice."

Another reality is that abortion is legal in this country, and will likely stay that way. Since we're realists, we would rather spend our time educating women about reasonable contraceptive choices than spend it trying to overturn *Roe v. Wade.* There's nothing we would love more than to drastically reduce the number of abortions in this country. We would like for women to understand what they're doing to their bodies and their unborn children when they're undergoing an abortion. We would like to see a bit of *shame* return to the idea of abortion. And we would like women to understand that abortion is anything but empowering. In fact, it's just the opposite.

. . . .

We would like to see a bit of *shame* return to the idea of abortion.

. . . .

The "common ground" Obama speaks of in the presidential campaign speech we mentioned earlier is pretty tough to find when one side believes in something so philosophically and morally different than the other. Obama may *say* that "nobody's pro-abortion," but a simple Google search on "guilt-free abortion" proves otherwise. So does a critical look at headlines over the past several years. Pro-abortion folks don't like considering what abortions really are—they're too busy fighting for ways to make it easier for women to have them without shame and without conscience. It's why they get really upset when they're faced with photographic evidence of abortion "remains." It's why they fight so hard against states requiring ultrasounds before abortions. Reality and pro-abortion folks just don't get along very well.

A Gallup poll in May 2013 showed that 48 percent of respondents identified themselves as pro-life, while 45 percent said they were pro-choice.[3] Isn't it interesting, then, that the mainstream media in America, largely controlled by the Left, focuses so much of its attention on the "pro-choice" crowd? They love to portray those kooky pro-lifers as the extremists. Pro-lifers are painted as shotgun-wielding, pickup driving, Bible-thumping wackjobs married to their first cousins, and just not as *enlightened* as the intellectually superior talking heads who believe in "choice."

It's really no wonder that many Americans are reluctant to associate themselves with the pro-life label. Because who wants to admit that they are against "choice," right? Similarly, though, nobody wants to say they're pro-abortion. That sounds positively horrible compared to being pro-choice. But contrary to what Dear Leader tells us, there are folks who make it their life's work to protect women's ability to kill their own children at any point in pregnancy. They're the people who won't rest until abortions are offered at Starbucks.

They're the people who fight tooth and nail to make sure that a dirty, disgusting clinic of horrors like Kermit Gosnell's in Philadelphia stays intact and operating.

KILLER GOSNELL AND HIS FRIEND CALLED MEDIA

We'd like to assume that everyone has heard of Kermit Gosnell, but because of a complicit lamestream media, we simply can't. Gosnell is the Philadelphia doctor who ran an abortion clinic called the Women's Medical Society, and while that seems like a distinguished name, it was anything but. In 2013, Gosnell was convicted of first-degree murder in the deaths of three babies whom he killed with scissors after they were delivered alive in that disgusting, dirty abortion clinic. He was also convicted of involuntary manslaughter in the case of a patient who died of a drug overdose after undergoing an abortion.[4] Gosnell murdered *thousands* of babies over the course of his thirty years in the abortion business in the neighborhood in which he grew up, and he made a very lucrative living doing so. In fact, authorities said that he raked in about $1.8 million a year after taxes, and they found a $250,000 stash of cash in one of Gosnell's bedrooms during a sweep of his home. He enjoyed a beach home and some lovely rental properties from the riches he made from drugging women and murdering babies in his abortion clinic, which has now been dubbed the House of Horrors.

In fact, in April 2013, Terry Moran, chief foreign correspondent for ABC News, described the abortionist best when he tweeted, "Kermit Gosnell is probably the most successful serial killer in the history of the world."

The case actually blew wide open back in 2011, but you probably didn't hear much about Kermit Gosnell at that time. You probably weren't aware that Gosnell's booming business was late-term abortions. And you probably didn't know that the success behind that business model was because according to the grand jury report:

> When you perform late-term "abortions" by inducing labor, you get babies. Live, breathing, squirming babies. By 24 weeks, most babies born prematurely will survive if they receive appropriate medical care. But that was not what the Women's Medical Society was about. Gosnell had a simple solution for the unwanted babies he delivered: he killed them. He didn't call it that. He called it "ensuring fetal demise." The way he ensured fetal demise was by sticking scissors into the back of the baby's neck and cutting the spinal cord. He called that "snipping."[5]

Evidently, there's a demand for this, and irresponsible chicks with big ol' unwanted, late-term babies in their bellies pay big money for "snipping."

You may have not heard much about Gosnell when he was convicted back in 2013, either, because the media was too busy shining spotlights on more important and newsworthy people and their fashion choices. You know, like Wendy Davis and her pink tennies. We're pretty certain that you *have* heard of Wendy and her famous footwear. Who hasn't, for crying out loud? Wendy's blond, pretty, petite, and we'd bet that the catheter she sported on the senate floor in Texas during her eleven-hour filibuster in 2013 against HB2—the legislation that mandated abortion clinics have the same standards as ambulatory surgical centers—was as couture as her Escada coat.

. . . .

Wendy's blond, pretty, petite, and we'd bet that the catheter she sported on the senate floor in Texas during her eleven-hour filibuster in 2013 against HB2—the legislation that mandated abortion clinics have the same standards as ambulatory surgical centers—was as couture as her Escada coat.

. . . .

Davis, a.k.a. "Abortion Barbie," has her sights set on climbing the public service ladder, and she announced a run for governor of that decidedly red state of Texas in late 2013. You see, Davis is to baby-killing what Sandra Fluke was to birth control, and she soon became Democrats' poster girl for abortion rights. But it seems that she, like many others in this country, relied on our media for her information about Gosnell, too. Because two months after sporting that catheter on the senate floor, she was asked about the difference between the late-term abortions she fought to keep legal in Texas and the illegal killings by Philadelphia abortionist Dr. Kermit Gosnell. And you know what she told the *Weekly Standard*'s John McCormack? She said, "I don't know what happened in the Gosnell case."[6]

Um, what? The politician who was the de facto poster woman for abortion rights didn't know what happened in the Gosnell case before she stood up to filibuster a bill that was written in *response* to the Gosnell case? Wouldn't it have made some sense for her to do some basic due diligence first?

There's this thing called Google, Wendy. You may want to look into it.

Because she's totally clueless, Davis continued with this doozy, which should make anyone who paid the slightest bit of attention to the Gosnell case shake their heads in amazement: "But I do know that [Gosnell] happened in an ambulatory surgical center. And in Texas changing our clinics to that standard obviously isn't going to make a difference."

Actually, Gosnell did *not* commit his atrocities in an ambulatory surgical center. And women died in his so-called care, in that barely regulated dumpy clinic, along with their babies. And according to the case's grand jury report, he "overdosed his patients with dangerous drugs, spread venereal disease among them with infected instruments, [and] perforated their wombs and bowels. . . . "[7] But listen, if Wendy said that standards in abortion clinics aren't important, then we should probably defer to the chick who got a feature story in *Vogue*, because she's, like, *totes adorbs*, right?

Welcome to the American media narrative, folks.

For those of us who knew what was going on in the Gosnell case—those of us who pay attention to alternative news sources, that is—we saw the horror that should have been covered on every "mainstream" news outlet in this country. But it wasn't. Most liberals were silent, but one *Huffington Post* host, Marc Lamont Hill, had the balls to at least say publicly what we conservatives knew all along back in April 2013:

> *For what it's worth, I do think that those of us on the left have made a decision not to cover this trial because we*

MOTHERHOOD IS NOT A DIRTY WORD

Mary Elizabeth Williams at *Salon* wrote a column about how a woman shouldn't revere motherhood as the most important role in her life, by criticizing Natalie Portman for having the *audacity* to show happiness about her pregnancy during her Oscar acceptance speech back in 2011.[8]

We are not making this up.

According to Mary Elizabeth Williams, you should be offended by Natalie's speech, because after she tearfully expressed gratitude to her co-nominees, her parents, her manager, her agent, her friends, her directors, her producers, her peers, and even her makeup-and-hair people, she thanked her partner: "My beautiful love, Benjamin, who choreographed the film, and who has now given me my most important role of my life."

This new role was motherhood, Portman being pregnant with their first child. Williams wrote, "At the time, the comment jarred me, as it does every time anyone refers to motherhood as the most important thing a woman can possibly do." The rest of Williams's column then addressed that particular sentence—her own. Not what Natalie Portman actually said, mind you, but the statement that "motherhood is the most important thing a woman can possibly do." Williams asked, "But is motherhood really a greater role than being secretary of state or a justice on the Supreme Court? Is reproduction automatically the greatest thing Natalie Portman will do with her life?"

This totally pissed us off. Natalie Portman never said that motherhood was the most important thing a woman can possibly do. She said it would be the most important role of *her* life. We fail to see why Williams could even *begin* to argue what priority level Natalie Portman gives her career versus her role as a mom.

But Williams continued being in a huff about it. She wrote, "Why, at the pinnacle of one's professional career, would a person feel the need to undercut it by announcing that there's something else even more important? Motherhood is important. So is work. And you don't have to backhandedly downplay one to be proud of the other."

Now, you could make a strong argument that motherhood truly is the most important role a woman will ever have. But we're not convinced that that's the main issue here. The main issue is that Williams *doesn't get to choose* what role Natalie Portman, or any other woman for that matter, values most.

Liberal feminists love to claim that they're all about freedom and choices, but the reality is that they only like choices when they've made them *for* you. The only real choice they like to talk about is the kind that ends a human life.

And that's our point. Liberal feminists can claim to be about choice all they want, but they're not.

Let's call pro-choice what it is. It's pro-abortion.

worry that it'll compromise abortion rights. Whether you agree with abortion or not, I do think there's a direct connection between the media's failure to cover this and our own political commitments on the left. I think it's a bad idea, I think it's dangerous, but I think that's the way it is.[9]

Yep. That's about right.

The truth is, pro-abortion folks don't want regulation of clinics or standards, because that might (gasp) limit access to abortions. Because who cares about details like safe clinics? Who needs high standards of care when it's "women's reproductive health" we're talking about? Why would any self-respecting woman want *that*? Republicans are such meanies for wanting to protect women from bleeding out on dirty tables and getting their wombs and bowels perforated and being cared for by unqualified, uncertified, uneducated staff, right?

Gosnell was indeed the most successful serial killer in history, and the media was a willing accomplice during his trial, as evidenced by too many people in this country being sorely uninformed about who he was and the barbaric things he did. But hey—thanks in part to our liberal American media—we can at least all rest easy with the *crucial* knowledge that Wendy McAbortionBarbie loves red wine and Lululemon yoga pants.

WHY YES, YOU SHOULD BE ASHAMED OF YOURSELF

As if ignoring something like the Gosnell case wasn't bad enough, liberals seem to have taken it upon themselves to make abortion into a badge of girl-power strength. In fact, it's like a feminist battle cry to be able to say, "I chose to kill my baby. I'm a martyr for the Democratic Party now. Can I have one of those nifty pink T-shirts with the oversized uterus on it now?" Liberal feminists have set out to make abortion an act of *courage* these days.

Granted, we recognize that for some women, the decision to abort a baby isn't one they make lightly at all. We empathize with women who make the agonizing decision to terminate their pregnancies when they find out the baby has trisomy 18 or other similar life-threatening conditions that will dramatically reduce the chance for that baby to have any decent quality of life. It's for precisely those reasons that we don't spend time advocating making abortion illegal. But we have no tolerance—absolutely none—for women who simply can't be bothered to be responsible about their own contraception and therefore use abortion as birth control. We want to see as few abortions as possible, and we'd really like to see a little *shame* return to the abortion business. Yup—we said it—*shame*. It certainly shouldn't be deemed heroic to end a baby's life, and women shouldn't be *applauded* for doing so. Guilt-free, shameless abortions are what liberals are peddling these days, and we find it not only vomit inducing, but also terrifying for humanity.

Case in point.

Beth Matusoff Merfish of the *New York Times* is one of those chicks who believes it's "brave" to use abortion as birth control. And let's face it: that's why most women get abortions these days. It's not because they were raped or because they were incest victims. In fact, less than 1 percent of all abortions are carried out because of rape or incest.[10] Beth's mom—Sherry Matusoff Merfish—had an abortion back in 1972, and because Beth has been brainwashed into thinking that abortion is some sort of rite of passage these days, she wrote a whole article in praise of her mom's "brave" decision.[11]

Keep in mind that Mrs. Merfish didn't have the abortion because her life was in danger or because she was raped or because she was a victim of incest or any of those so-called acceptable reasons that seem to be used as the overwhelming reason why abortions are so necessary. Nope. She used abortion as a form of *birth control, just as thousands of other women do.* She was twenty, her fiancé (and father of the unborn baby) was twenty-one, and they felt "thoroughly unprepared" to be parents. They were afraid of their family's reaction to finding out they'd engaged in premarital sex. And yet, her actions were described in the article with words like "courage" and "bravery." She killed her unborn baby instead of facing the disappointment of her family and accepting the consequences of her actions, which would have been, incidentally, the far more courageous and brave thing to do.

Beth concluded her article with this (emphasis ours):

> **The opposition is frightening,** *as more states try to restrict abortion, but there is tremendous power and safety in numbers. You are part of a society of women who have been incredibly courageous; I ask humbly for yet another show of that bravery.*

Did you catch that load of horse crap? That is some serious crazy right there. "The opposition is frightening"?

You know what's actually frightening? A human being getting a blade rammed into its spinal cord.

You know what *else* is frightening? Abortion clinics that look like Kermit Gosnell's, where substandard care for women is the norm, where doctors aren't required to meet the same health and safety regulations as an ambulatory surgical center, and where—come to think of it—you don't even need a doctor to perform the procedure at all.[12] Hell, just get a *nail technician* to do it. Oh wait, they have *more* regulations at nail salons. We forgot.

A return to shame would be a step in the right direction for those of us who respect and revere human life. After all, it *should* be shameful to end a life, shouldn't it? It's why conservatives are right to believe that legislation that requires a woman to have an ultrasound before aborting her baby is appropriate. It's why conservatives are right to believe that requiring women to go through at least minimal counseling about alternatives to abortion is appropriate. Abortions shouldn't be easy and convenient. They should be heartbreaking, agonizing, and rare last resorts. It is shameful to callously and willfully end a human life. Unfortunately, it's difficult to attach shame to something that liberals make sound like an advertisement for a tampon commercial.

FROM PRO-CHOICE TO PRO-LIFE: AN AMY JO STORY

When Miriam and I first started our site more than four years ago, she had always been pro-life, but I called myself pro-choice. I dug my heels in on the whole pro-choice label mainly because I was sorely uninformed about abortion (I admit that openly now). Yes, I have ladyparts, even though I hate that stupid word. And yes, I've understood where babies have come from since my sister told me all about it when I was a little girl. And yes, I also believe in God. But up until I actually got pregnant in my late thirties, I didn't think much about abortion. I just always called myself pro-choice and avoided it. It was easier that way, you see.

Then we started our site. I read. I became informed. I got involved. I immersed myself in the political machine more so than ever before in my life and I was thrown into a discussion that I never had to actively participate in before. I mean, I've always been a conservative, but I'd never had to really *think* about abortion myself, because I've never wanted or needed one. God knows I'd never have one myself—it simply goes against everything I believe in. But I always said to myself, *Who am I to tell a woman who's been raped or a victim of incest that she can't have one, right?* I was like a lot of folks: I simply wanted to label it as a *choice*. Not a *murder*. I wanted to believe it was some sort of *freedom* for a woman. And I'm all about freedom. Freedom is a *good* thing, after all.

. . . .

The silver lining in those lost pregnancies is that I saw the truth. Life is kind of awesome that way—sometimes it slaps you around to make you see things that were obvious all along but you were just too flipping blind to see.

. . . .

Then I got pregnant, three times, actually. I lost the first two pregnancies, and I mourned those lost pregnancies. I still do. I learned quickly that I was one of those women who became a mom the day I learned I was pregnant. It's as simple and as complicated as that.

The silver lining in those lost pregnancies is that I saw the truth. Life is kind of awesome that way—sometimes it slaps you around to make you see things that were obvious all along but you were just too flipping blind to see. It took me about thirty-nine years to say that I am pro-life, but when someone asks me now, I do say (out loud and everything), "Yeah, I'm pro-life." Even three years ago, it would've felt weird to own the label "pro-life." But today? It fits like a glove.

If you're like I was, you should try it on for size. What's the alternative, after all? Saying you're pro-choice? For what? Ending a life? Is that what you're choosing? Because when faced with that question—when someone actually *asked* me what I was choosing when I was pro-choice—I knew deep down that I wasn't pro-choice at all. I was just avoiding the discussion. I was just taking the easy way out.

It took losing those pregnancies—hearing the heartbeats for each one of them, feeling life inside of me three different times, and seeing that last little heartbeat grow into the miracle standing in front of me today as a young, thriving girl—for me to say out loud that abortion is the farthest thing from freedom. It's not a choice at all. It *is* the ending of a human life. Plain and simple, and there's no amount of avoidance or explanation or rationalization or semantic two-stepping that can make it otherwise. As uncomfortable and unpleasant as that may be for those who still want to label it as a choice or a freedom, well, *tough*. There is no gray. It's black and white. It's life or death. And I absolutely wish that clarity for other people.

CHAPTER 10

We Are Pro-Contraception and Pro–Plan B

Contraception has become a tricky topic for pro-life folks. Birth control pills, which have been widely used by thousands and thousands of women in the United States for decades, are now the subject of hot debate in many religious circles. And when you throw emergency contraception like Plan B into the conversation, the debate gets even hotter. Truth be told, our own position about contraception has evolved quite substantially as we've become more informed, but we've always been convinced of one thing: if our ultimate goal is to drastically reduce the number of abortions that occur every single year, we must exercise some flexibility in our tolerance of contraception (and even emergency contraception). After doing a lot of research and soul-searching, we are now firmly in the pro-contraception and pro–Plan B camp.

Some of you conservatives probably have your feathers all ruffled now. You're about to call us RINOs and just toss this book aside. We are conservative, and we support the use of birth control pills and even Plan B.

Just hear us out on this, folks.

HOW EMERGENCY CONTRACEPTION WORKS

In the interest of full disclosure here, you should know that until relatively recently, we were pretty conflicted about birth control pills and particularly Plan B emergency contraception, because a lot of literature (including the product packaging for those contraceptives) described one of the pregnancy-prevention mechanisms of oral birth control as "preventing the implantation of a fertilized egg in the uterus by altering its lining." In fact, the Plan B website explains,

> *Plan B One-Step® contains a higher dose of levonorgestrel than birth control pills, but works in a similar way to prevent pregnancy. It works mainly by stopping the release of an egg from the ovary. It is possible that Plan B One-Step® may also work by preventing fertilization of an egg (the uniting of sperm with the egg) or by preventing attachment (implantation) to the uterus (womb).[1]*

It was our view that any contraceptive that worked by preventing implantation of a fertilized egg was an abortifacient. But according to Physicians for Reproductive Health, the American Congress of Obstetricians and Gynecologists, the American Society for Reproductive Medicine, the National Association of Nurse Practitioners in Women's Health, the International Association of Forensic Nurses, and the American College of Nurse-Midwives, and many other associations of professionals who should know, this is not the case. (And if you want to believe that all of these organizations are conspiring to trick women into having abortions, then be our guest.)

According to the brief of amici curiae from the aforementioned groups:

The medical and scientific record establishes that the emergency contraceptives approved by the FDA . . . do not interfere with pregnancy and are not abortifacients, because they are not effective after a fertilized egg has successfully implanted in the uterus." [2]

And furthermore:

Abortifacient has a precise meaning in the medical and scientific community and it refers to the termination of a pregnancy. Contraceptives that prevent fertilization from occurring, or even prevent implantation, are simply not abortifacients regardless of an individual's personal or religious beliefs or mores.

This was a bit of a revelation for us.

In fact, when we read that only around 40 percent of fertilized eggs ever implant into the uterus naturally, we gained a lot of clarity about the entire contraception versus abortifacient issue. In the medical and scientific community, pregnancy begins once a blastocyst (fertilized egg) has implanted into the uterus. This definition of pregnancy is not only accepted by all major U.S. medical organizations and governmental agencies, but it's also the legal definition of pregnancy as well.

According to the same group of aforementioned medical organizations, the product label for Plan B has not been updated since the product was originally approved in 1999. This kind of sucks, actually, because it doesn't reflect the most recent research or studies, the most relevant of which indicate that Plan B *doesn't* prevent implantation of a fertilized egg. But even if emergency contraception did prevent implantation, it would still not be categorized as an abortifacient.

Put simply, contraceptives prevent pregnancies. Abortifacients terminate them. Neither birth control pills nor emergency contraceptives work to terminate pregnancies.

And this is why we support contraception and Plan B.

WHEN DOES LIFE BEGIN?

"But Chicks!" some folks will say. *"Life begins at conception!!"*

If you are adamantly opposed to all forms of synthetic hormone contraception or IUDs because of the very unlikely possibility that those forms of birth control could prevent a fertilized egg from implanting into the uterus, we congratulate you on your purism, but we ask you how you're actually helping the cause to reduce the number of abortions. Because if you're expecting that every American is going to limit her contraception method to either condoms or the practice of "natural family planning," and you also expect that this thinking is somehow going to result in a decrease in abortion, then with all due respect, you are high.

If you're internally conflicted about this, you're not alone. The morality aspect of birth control pills is an ever-growing controversy among Christians.[3] However, many self-proclaimed pro-life women (us included) are either currently on some sort of birth control or have taken birth control pills at some point in their lives. According to the CDC and a study they did of 65 million American women, 55 percent of those between the ages of 20 and 24 use contraception, while 78 percent of those between the ages of 25 and 44 do. Among women under 30, "a higher percentage of women used the pill than any other method."[4]

. . . .

Mourning the loss of thousands of unimplanted fertilized eggs seems completely counterproductive considering that thousands of fully formed fetuses with beating hearts are killed every single day.

. . . .

That's a lot of women on birth control in this country. You may actually be one of them. And our clarity on this issue comes from the fact that pregnancy doesn't actually begin until a fertilized egg implants into the womb (which, again, happens less than 50 percent of the time naturally to begin with). Mourning the loss of thousands of unimplanted fertilized eggs seems completely counterproductive considering that thousands of fully formed fetuses with beating hearts are killed every single day.

If your definition of abortion includes every instance of a fertilized egg failing to implant in the uterus, then you're essentially suggesting that millions of women are murderers without even realizing it.

We simply cannot agree with that. This is why we accept the legal, medically accepted definition of pregnancy.

That's also what really bothers us about any kind of legislation that bestows all of the legal and constitutional attributes and privileges of personhood to one-celled human embryos that haven't even implanted into the uterus yet (as Rep. Paul Broun's proposed bill aimed to do in 2011).[5] Because not only are bills like that completely absurd and impossible to regulate or enforce in any way, but they also eliminate the choice women currently have to use IUDs, regular birth control pills, and even in vitro fertilization.

We realize this is all pretty technical, scientific stuff. But we point these things out simply to make sure that before people yell at us for saying that we're not really pro-life because we support birth control and Plan B, they first realize the full weight of what they are saying and understand that if *they* are drawing the line at the moment of fertilization, they are effectively saying that birth control pills and IUDs should be every bit as immoral as the act that we normally think of when we mention the word "abortion." We think that's pretty unreasonable.

MAKING THE BEST OF A BAD SITUATION

We despise the fact that abortion has become so easy, so convenient, and so absolutely the hallmark of liberal feminists that it has become its own legitimate form of birth control. That's beyond sickening. Women need to be responsible enough so that if they intend to have sex, and if they do not want to become pregnant, they should take steps before sexual activity to make sure that they are protected. This isn't rocket science. But as realists, we understand that people don't always make good decisions. While we don't condone emergency contraception as a form of birth control, we'd rather see a woman at the pharmacy getting Plan B the morning after she has unprotected sex than having an abortion well into her first, second, or third trimester of pregnancy. Wouldn't every pro-life person prefer that? We don't live in an ideal world. So shouldn't we exercise some tolerance about contraceptive solutions in order to ensure later-term abortions are as rare as possible?

We must recognize and accept the fact that abortion is legal. We don't see a lot of indication that it's going to ever be made *illegal*. In other words, outrage about abortions, by itself, *won't stop abortions*. And neither will opposition to forms of contraception that, in all likelihood, *prevent* a huge number of abortions. We believe conservatives should focus on tangible areas where we can make some actual headway on this issue. While we love the idea of simply teaching our kids abstinence and promoting sex within the confines of a committed marriage, that's not necessarily realistic. To us, it makes more sense to fight for the baby steps (no pun intended). We believe that what could help abortions become more rare (which is what all of us want) is balanced encouragement of birth control options and a broader tolerance of emergency contraception, particularly if it will prevent later-term abortions. As we stated in the "We Are Pro-Life" chapter, we are in favor of the legislation that liberals bitch about that makes it less convenient than it currently is to get an abortion. We're in favor of legislation that requires women to have an ultrasound to see exactly what they're about to do before they have an abortion. And absolutely, we're in favor of emergency contraception like the morning-after or Plan B pill, in part because emergency contraception eliminates the whole "But what about cases of rape and incest?" argument. There is absolutely no reason in the world that a victim of rape or incest should need to wait to terminate a pregnancy well into the first trimester (or beyond)—ever. And if you think about it, there's no reason anyone else should either.

It's old news by now that a federal judge ordered the government to remove all obstacles to over-the-counter sales of Plan B. Administration policy is that children as young as fifteen can buy the drug without a prescription or parental knowledge. There is talk that the age restriction may be removed altogether.

Many conservatives are, of course, outraged by this, and in many ways we share the outrage. A teen can't get a freaking Tylenol from the school nurse without parental approval, but if she wants to walk into a CVS to buy Plan B, it's completely fine? Whizzah?

But here's the thing. No teenage girl is going to go into a drugstore to buy Plan B unless she has a reason to. Does it completely blow chunks that we live in a world where fifteen-year-old girls (and younger) are sexually active? Yup. Is this law going to change that for better or for worse? Nope.

We agree with Kathleen Parker of the *Washington Post*, who said that we should involve and not marginalize parents.[6] We agree that government should have a limited involvement in our lives. We agree that parents should have ultimate authority over their children's well-being. *Hello*, we are conservatives, for crying out loud.

But then there's that whole realism thing. We know that if we had a teenage daughter who had just had unprotected sex, we would hope she'd talk to us about it immediately. And what we'd likely do is tell her to take the Plan B pill, and then promptly make sure she got on regular birth control pills. If our relationship wasn't conducive to that kind of self-disclosure on her part, we'd hope she would take the Plan B pill on her own, immediately after having unprotected sex, instead of waiting and deciding later to get an abortion without telling us. Because in that situation, in which every solution is less than ideal, a later-term abortion would be the most devastating solution of all.

So do we think the Plan B pill should be available to girls as young as fifteen without parental consent? Well, based on the previous dialogue, we guess our answer is ultimately *yes*. Because as much as we loathe the idea, we would rather a fifteen-year-old girl who doesn't have a close relationship with her parents take that precautionary step versus the worse alternative, which might be an abortion later on in an established pregnancy. It's the lesser of two evils, frankly.

Conservatives are right to have high moral standards, but we're also right to avoid damaging our own causes with impossibly unrealistic goals. And we're right to make strides in this movement in the best, most realistic ways that we possibly can.

CHAPTER 11

We Don't Care Whom You Sleep With

Here's a newsflash. We don't give two craps about whom you sleep with. We don't care about your gayness, your straightness, your bi-curiousness, your asexuality, or your transsexuality. Your sexuality is of absolutely no consequence to us. What gets to us, though, are people who define themselves *by* their sexuality. In the same way we get annoyed by feminists who define themselves by their ladyparts, we take issue with gay people who cannot see outside the prism of their own sexuality. This is why you'll often hear us say, "That's great that you're gay, but no one cares. Just be gay and stop making it the cornerstone of your entire existence already."

This will probably make liberals' heads explode (and maybe even some conservatives' heads, too!), but we have LGBT friends and followers who are conservative. So let's just make sure this point is getting across: LGBT conservatives exist. And you know what else? Even LGBT *Christian* conservatives exist.

Conservatives are right to love their LGBT conservative brothers and sisters. Because conservatives, no matter what their sexual preference or orientation, typically *don't* obsess over their sexuality. They're too busy focusing on issues that matter. And for people on the left to try to compartmentalize and segregate and claim that LGBT conservatives don't exist? To deny that our LGBT friends are as conservative as they claim? To accuse them of being sellouts? That's not very "progressive," now, is it?

Conservatives are right to react against arguments that reduce human beings to whom they sleep with. We're right to believe that people with different beliefs about sexual orientation can coexist. We're right to want conservatives to choose their battles, and we're right to believe that people deserve the space to figure out their own beliefs without being marginalized as bigots.

LOOK AT ME! I'M GAY!

For being such a small segment of society, the LGBT community makes *a lot* of noise. For example, they have organized gay-pride parades all over the country—all over the world, in fact—to celebrate their gayness. And the LGBT acronym is growing longer. Now LGBTQIA, it stands for lesbian, gay and/or genderqueer, bisexual, transgender and/or transsexual, questioning and/or queer, intersex, and ally and/or asexual.

We're not making that up. By the time you sit down to read this book, in fact, every letter of the alphabet might well be represented.

While people who are gay or bisexual or questioning or intersex or *whatever* are certainly free to classify themselves in whatever way they choose, we're not entirely sure why their nontraditional sexual preferences are a source of *pride*. Why is being gay something to be celebrated with a parade?

Perhaps it sounds harsh, but being LGBTQIA doesn't make you special. It doesn't make you worthy of extra attention or deserving of recognition or entitled to acceptance by others.

Unfortunately, though, many people in the LGBT community base their entire identities around their sexual preferences. And invariably, these are the people who are the most insufferable. They're the ones who behave like depraved animals in those gay-pride parades. They're the ones who sue Christian photographers for not wanting to photograph their same-sex wedding. They're the ones who don't just demand tolerance; they demand to be adored and praised for their bravery for being gay.

It doesn't help that we now live in a culture where "coming out" as a gay person is applauded as some sort of incredible achievement. Take basketball player Jason Collins, for example.

Jason Collins, an NBA basketball player, became the first openly gay male athlete in major professional team sports in 2013 by writing a piece for the April issue of *Sports Illustrated* that year. He wrote, "I'm a 34-year-old NBA center. I'm black. And I'm gay."[1]

Judging by the reaction to this earth-shattering announcement, you'd have thought he'd just cured cancer or something, because that proclamation prompted a personal phone call to Jason from President Obama himself.[2] The First Lady tweeted to Jason, "So proud of you, Jason Collins! We've got your back!" He was described as courageous and brave. *Just because he sleeps with other dudes, and decided to tell everyone about it.* That's what classifies as courageous and brave now.

Wow.

THE PLIGHT OF THE LGBT CONSERVATIVE

Meanwhile, on the other end of the spectrum, there are the LGBT folks who, like most straight people, quietly love whom they love and don't feel a need to be in everyone's face about it. They know that their sexual preference is mostly irrelevant in the grand scheme of things. It doesn't consume them. We've become acquainted with several LGBT folks through our website and so-cial media platforms, and they've sought us out because they're conservative, and they feel like they don't belong anywhere. The reason? Many liberals don't believe that people can be gay, bisex-ual, or transsexual and conservative at the same time. Appar-ently, in the broader LGBT community, if you don't vote Democrat, you're simply not LGBT *enough*. It's the same mental-ity of liberals who accuse conservative women of being anti-woman. If we have vaginas, then we're apparently automatically supposed to be liberals, because *War on Women*! Or something.

This is the stereotype that the Left thrives on perpetuating—that LGBT people *can't* be con-servative.

This is the stereotype that the Left thrives on perpetuating—that LGBT people *can't* be conservative. That's the narrative they want to force down your throat. And when LGBT conser-vatives push back? Well, they're often attacked, demeaned, and discounted.

If you visit gayconservative.org, for example, there's a note written to liberals who happen to land there that reads in part:

The most frequent comment we hear is, "how can you be gay and be politically conservative?!?" That is generally fol-lowed by every political slur in the liberal vernacular—idiot, moron, brainwashed, traitor, deviant, and the ever-popular "self-loathing closet case." If you have a comment along those lines, then with all the respect we can offer, please stow it. We've heard it quite enough.[3]

They experience liberal tolerance in much the same way we do, it appears. And they answer the question "How can you be gay and be politically conservative?" in much the same way we answer the question "How can you be female and be politically conservative?" We all say, in essence, that the answer is quite simple. Conservative ideas make sense. We believe in limited government, power of the people, individual liberty, and a free market.

We're beyond proud of LGBT people who stick to their conservative guns. It'd be so much easier for them to conform—to jump on the liberal bandwagon, vote Democrat, and not deal with the constant backlash they get for being conservative. But they don't. They make the choice to be true to themselves and their conservative beliefs, because they know that their sexuality doesn't define them. They're better than that. And they understand that conservatism is common sense.

DUCKS, GAYS, AND COEXISTING

Back in December 2013, *Duck Dynasty*'s patriarch, Phil Robertson, was all the mainstream media could talk about after he was placed on "indefinite leave" from his family's reality show by A&E. The reason for the dismissal? Because he dared to express his Christian beliefs in an interview with *GQ* magazine.

If you lived under a rock during that time and are not aware of Phil's personal views, they included the following:

Start with homosexual behavior and just morph out from there. Bestiality, sleeping around with this woman and that woman and that woman and those men. Don't be deceived. Neither the adulterers, the idolaters, the male prostitutes, the homosexual offenders, the greedy, the drunkards, the slanderers, the swindlers—they won't inherit the kingdom of God. Don't deceive yourself. It's not right.

He also said about homosexuality:

It seems like, to me, a vagina—as a man—would be more desirable than a man's anus. That's just me. I'm just thinking: There's more there! She's got more to offer. I mean, come on, dudes! You know what I'm saying? But hey, sin: It's not logical, my man. It's just not logical.[4]

Upon reading this, GLAAD (Gay and Lesbian Alliance Against Defamation)—who had about seven hundred voting members at the time—completely wigged out about Phil's comments, saying that they were "some of the vilest and most extreme statements uttered against LGBT people in a mainstream publication" and that "his quote was littered with outdated stereotypes and blatant misinformation." They said:

Phil and his family claim to be Christian, but Phil's lies about an entire community fly in the face of what true Christians believe. . . . He clearly knows nothing about gay people or the majority of Louisianans—and Americans— who support legal recognition for loving and committed gay and lesbian couples. Phil's decision to push vile and extreme stereotypes is a stain on A&E and his sponsors, who now need to reexamine their ties to someone with such public disdain for LGBT people and families.[5]

And then the drama ensued. And ensued a bit more. And holy crap, ensued some more.

The fact that Phil was booted was the news of that month. No lie. It became bigger than any economic news, bigger than all of the scandals that were plaguing the White House (IRS targeting of Tea Party groups and Benghazi, for example), and bigger than even Obamacare—which was at the height of its disastrous implementation. *Duck Dynasty* saturated the news media, and it even took over social media. People were standing in solidarity with Phil by adorning themselves with beards (there was even an app for that!), and hashtags were created in support of both sides.

It was freaking ridiculous.

By far the most ridiculous part of the story is that what Duck dude actually said is the biggest nonnews ever. Phil believes homosexuality is a sin. So what? So do a zillion other people. He just happened to say it out loud—not even while on the show, mind you—and *boom*: it was the biggest news of the day. A fireable offense, even.

The bottom line is that A&E the *company* had the right to run their outfit however they wanted to. Suspending Phil Robertson from the show was a boneheaded move, and it ended up coming back to bite them in a big way. The Robertson clan stood by their father, and after the dust settled, the network realized that the show made them a lot of cash, and they reinstated Phil, because—go figure—money talks.

But you know what we learned from that whole fiasco? If you disagree with gayness in this country, you do so at your peril, people. We're pretty certain that if Phil had come out of the closet as a gay person instead of professing his religious beliefs, he'd be revered and praised and probably get a spin-off show, because the 3 percent of the U.S. population that's gay apparently has a stranglehold on the entertainment world. Meh, screw the Christians. Nowadays, it's all the rage to be gay, or at least to be *vocally* pro-gay. If your faith dictates you feel otherwise, you better just keep it to yourself. That's the message in America these days.

We love gay people, know gay people, and don't really care about their gayness one way or another. We also love and know people who feel exactly like Phil Robertson about homosexuality. We're not sure when our society got its panties so twisted that these two groups of people can't coexist in the media, and in the public eye, the same way that people do in actual life, but that's clearly where we are. And if you ask us, we all need to do a better job of choosing our battles.

CHOOSING OUR BATTLES: ONE MILLION MOMS VS. ELLEN DEGENERES

One Million Moms is a conservative group of women working to keep the media family friendly. Back in 2012, they took on J. C. Penney, because the retail chain has Ellen DeGeneres as a spokesperson. They were offended not because she says anything off-putting in the commercial, but simply because she's a lesbian.

Now, this kind of stuff is what makes us want to take some stock in Advil. Because as conservative chicks, we stand in the middle of Stereotype Road here, which is a weird place to be some days. Mainly because we're not dressed for it. No, seriously. Our shoes are not comfortable at all, and we stick out like sore thumbs.

On the other side of the perpetual-victim-because-I'm-gay coin, we have the Republican-mom stereotype to deal with. That stereotype is why we *do* have to give our stance on sexuality and how it somehow relates to politics. It's because of groups like One Million Moms that we Chicks are called homophobes on a regular basis. After all, we're conservative

Republicans, and we're moms, so we must hate the fact that a gay chick is in a J. C. Penney ad. Right?

Right?

Wrong. We simply don't care what Ellen DeGeneres chooses to do in her bedroom. And frankly, we remember thinking that the ad was marginally cute. We didn't take offense to it at all.

Sure, we can see how One Million Moms would see a need to criticize a show on MTV or some smut-laden commercial during prime time. Good for them. Seriously. We applaud them for calling out the trash on MTV, truth be told, as that network is a raging STD in multimedia format. And we'll freely admit that we loathe about 90 percent of the trash shoved down our collective throat on television these days, too. So they're not alone, and we aren't trying to diminish their overall mission.

The point here is that there are a whole mess of other things in the world that require conservative attention—attention from One Million Moms banding together as only mothers could, really. Mothers are a fierce bunch and pack a mean wallop. And we're pretty positive that a whole group of them could make a serious dent in helping our cause—in giving conservatism a much-needed makeover and reformulating our messaging. Which is perhaps more meaningful than trying to get a lesbian out of a J. C. Penney commercial.

Because seriously, has anyone even noticed that the freaking Kardashians have practically taken over the Sears brand? *Hello.*

Ellen responded to this nonissue with the following. And she has a really good point:

"I mean, if they have a problem with spokespeople, what about the Pillsbury Doughboy? I mean, he runs around without any pants on and basically begging people to poke his belly. What kind of message is that?"

Ellen was right.

When choosing our battles? This isn't one of them, folks.

TO PHOTOGRAPH OR NOT PHOTOGRAPH A GAY COUPLE . . . THAT IS THE QUESTION

Here's a battle that is worth fighting. In August 2013, the New Mexico Supreme Court ruled that a Christian wedding photographer had violated the state's human rights law by refusing to photograph a same-sex commitment ceremony.

You see, the photographers are Christian and don't believe in gay marriage and didn't want to take on that particular client. So they didn't. And the lesbians got upset. All hell broke loose, and the ruling posed a whole new set of questions. One of which was, do gay rights take priority over religious liberties? Ken Klukowski, the director for the Center for Religious Liberty at the conservative Family Research Council said it best:

> This decision would stun the framers of the U.S. Constitution, is a gross violation of the First Amendment, and should now be taken up by the U.S. Supreme Court to reaffirm the basic principle that the fundamental rights of free speech and the free exercise of religion do not stop at the exit door of your local church, and instead extend to every area of a religious person's life.[6]

As it turns out, according to a Rasmussen poll, 85 percent of folks in this country believe that the photographer actually *did* have a right to turn down the same-sex couple as a client.[7] But no matter, because the courts found this case to be more about *discrimination* than anything else. And discrimination won. It usually does. Because *Amerika*.

In this instance, the photographer declined to provide her services to a gay couple due to her religious beliefs, but as business owners, who's to say that she might not turn down another couple, just because she thinks the groom is a complete douche bag? God knows we would. That would be one of the perks of being an entrepreneur and owning your own business and determining whom you want to have as clients, right? See, we believe in that whole freedom thing and think people scream "*Discrimination!*" way too much and are perpetually over-offended and over-victimized in this country. It's why stores can say stuff like, "No shirt, no shoes, no service." You know.

Look, we're not photographers, and thank God for that, because we'd apparently be unemployed at this point, simply for not wanting to photograph people with bad breath or something, because we are supposed to have the choice to do so in a free America. What we are, though, is two conservative women who know that gay rights should never be used to infringe on religious liberty. That's a battle we won't stop fighting.

THE CHICKS' OFFICIAL GAY MARRIAGE STANCE

We'll be honest here: we avoided the "Where do you stand on gay marriage?" question for a long time before finally addressing it on our website. The reason for that was that we found ourselves feeling majorly conflicted about it. At some point, we realized it was perfectly OK to feel conflicted, and we realized that we certainly weren't alone in feeling conflicted. In fact, as conservatives who believe strongly in family and marriage, but who also feel compassion for our gay friends, it makes all the sense in the world to have mixed feelings about this complicated social issue.

While we're conflicted in what the best answer is with respect to gay marriage, what we're not conflicted about is how completely pissed off we get when people make assumptions about what we think about gay marriage. And that goes for conservatives and liberals alike. Just because we pull the Republican levers at the polling booth doesn't mean that we necessarily toe the party line on every single issue, nor does it mean all Republicans in general are in lockstep on every single issue. It's normal and human to have a certain level of uncertainty about deeply complex social issues.

We've had plenty of conversations about the gay marriage debate, and what we've come to realize above all else is that gay marriage is pretty much last on the list of our political concerns. We know it's one of the "hot-button" social issues that is fiercely argued over between conservatives and liberals, but as much as some conservatives think we *should* care about gay marriage, we simply have too many other important things to care about. If one of our gay friends got married, fine. That's awesome for them. They should just go register at freaking Crate and Barrel and get on with it already. But if they start demanding that churches be forced to marry them, then we're going to have a problem.

As much as some conservatives think we *should* care about gay marriage, we simply have too many other important things to care about.

What's amazing to us is the energy that goes into this entire gay marriage debate. Months ago, there was a huge Facebook campaign where people all over the country changed their profile photos to display the red equal sign in support of gay marriage. That equal sign was positively everywhere. We would love to see the same Facebook-profile-picture-bandwagon-passion in this country about Obamacare or the NSA spying on us or the hundreds of thousands of babies being murdered every year or the government trampling on our constitutional rights left and right. Where's the universal symbol we can display on our Facebook profiles for that stuff? Anyone? Bueller?

We mentioned earlier that we're conflicted about this issue. We would feel pretty safe betting that many other conservatives face the same sort of internal wrestling on gay marriage as we do. Because if we really break it down, our thought process looks like the chart on the next page.

You see? Lots of internal conflict on this. And when you add kids into the mix? Well, that's icing on the internal-conflict cake. There's a part of us that thinks, "Kids need a mom and a dad," but then we look at all of the messed-up kids out there, and we think, "Hello. Lindsay Lohan has a mom and a dad, and she's a walking nightmare and would probably be better off with five random drag queens and a rabid badger raising her." We're fully aware that there are plenty of committed, loving gay couples who would provide far better homes for kids than a lot of crazy straight parents.

We also think about how complicated this issue already is for schools, and how much modification and sidestepping there already is to make sure that nontraditional families are made to feel just as normal as traditional families. Again, we're talking about 3 to 5 percent of the population that we're essentially having to bend over backward for. And it makes us wonder sometimes, where does it end?

And in case you're wondering, this isn't a religious issue for us. We get that it *is* for lots of people (believe us, we see all of the scripture being posted on our Facebook wall by

PROCESS CHART

Government shouldn't be involved in marriage at all.

Government is involved in marriage, so because of that, the government should grant the same equal rights to gay people to enjoy the same equal benefits of marriage that straight people have.

We don't see why so many gays are so adamant about having to change the definition of marriage. Marriage is defined as being between a man and a woman. So, we get a little prickly about the name.

At the same time, we think, "Why should we care if they call themselves married or not? How does this affect us? And then we kinda think it doesn't affect us.

We're convinced that the traditional family breakdown is one of the primary reasons our country is so completely messed up right now.
And the acceptance of homosexuality as "normal" has a role to play in that.
Because as much as we love our gay friends, there is still that traditional part of us that thinks it's NOT normal. It's different, and even though we love gay people as much as we love straight people, it's simply not how nature intended for things to be.

We believe that gay people are born gay. Because why on earth would anyone choose to be gay? That said, people are born in lots of ways that aren't "normal." And we can't think of a single other minority group (because let's face it—gay people make up somewhere between 3-5% of the American population) which makes this much noise and demands this much attention and this much accommodation. Which is why we're always saying, "We don't care if you're gay. But for crying out loud, just be gay and shut up about it already."

well-intentioned fellow conservatives who basically tell us that we're going to hell for even showing kindness to the LGBT community), and we understand that of course there are religious implications here. We respect that. However, our stance is that we don't presume to determine how God might judge others' sins, since we are all sinners. This is why you won't ever see us quoting Bible verses to defend conservative principles. We personally believe in God and are Christians, but conservatism as an ideology is strong enough to stand on its own without leaning on religion to prop up its arguments.

So there you have it. We are just incredibly conflicted. But what we're not conflicted about is equal rights for couples, no matter whether they're gay or straight. Civil unions for everyone, in fact, if government must be involved. And then marriage through the church, and *definitely* no forcing churches to marry gay couples if that's not in line with their religious principles. If gay people who are united civilly want to call themselves "married," then you know what? We don't care. But there is absolutely no reason for them to insist that the 95 percent of the rest of the country that isn't gay call it "marriage." Because while gay people are entitled to equal rights and equal opportunities, they are most certainly not entitled to be embraced by others, or liked by others, or even accepted by others. Because *no one* is.

The bottom line here is that conservatives are right to be critical of people who demand social approval and acceptance, when those are things that aren't owed to anyone. We're right to be critical of those in the LGBT community who discount and devalue LGBT conservatives.

We are also right to recognize that within conservatism, there is room for people like us—people who are conflicted about gay marriage—just as much as there's room for those who are squarely opposed to it for various reasons, including

While gay people are entitled to equal rights and equal opportunities, they are most certainly not entitled to be embraced by others, or liked by others, or even accepted by others. Because *no one* is.

THE HYPOCRITICAL HILARITY OF LIBERALS

It has become a hilarious part of the official liberal insult playbook to accuse us of being lesbians as a way of trying to hurt us somehow. Every time one of these jokers comes to our Facebook page and vomits this lame crap onto our wall, we just sigh, shake our heads, and wonder if there's a class they all take together or something that causes this ridiculous groupthink mentality they've got going on.

The level of offense we take to being called lesbians is exactly the same as the level of offense we'd take to being otherwise accused of something that is simply not true. It's like them saying, "The Chicks each have seven pinkie toes!" If it were true, we'd be more than delighted to say, "Why yes! *Yes, we do have seven pinkie toes!*" But we don't. If we were lesbians, we would be more than delighted to say, "Why yes! *Yes, we are lesbians!*" We would own it. And that's what's so funny about the insults (veiled or otherwise) that these people throw at us. All their accusations do is shine a big, bright light on their own hatred toward gay people. Because if they thought it was acceptable and awesome to be gay, then why would they use that as an insult? Right?

religious ones. Because conservatism is about far more than whom we choose to love.

Instead of wasting energy worrying about to whom other people are sexually attracted, conservatives would spend their time far more effectively by acknowledging that regardless of sexual preference, all couples should have the same civil rights, privileges, and benefits, particularly when it comes to wills, hospital visitations, and so on. That's a no-brainer. But more importantly, all of us—regardless of sexual orientation—should be focusing on the fact that our free-market society is at risk, our constitutional freedoms are continuously diluted by an overreaching government, and our American liberties are at stake. Those are the burning houses that require emergency attention. The question of whether or not gay people should be "married" is simply a distraction—a broken window in a burning house. We're right to expect conservatives to choose their battles wisely. Let's focus on putting out the fire.

CHAPTER 12

It's Time for a Conservative Makeover

It's not cool to be conservative these days. The lamestream media tells us that all the time. We're tempted to say that doesn't matter, but it does. While we conservatives might find it distasteful and tedious to play the popularity game, it's a game that we *must* play well if we are to win elections. It's not about wanting to be the cool kids on the block; it's about recognizing that perception becomes reality. If liberals continue to succeed with their categorization of conservatives as old, stodgy white dudes, then we don't have a snowball's chance in hell of making headway. We recognize that strong, effective conservative messaging requires a few fresh ingredients to make the best possible special sauce: optimism, realness, relevance, courage, and conviction—and then that awesomesauce needs to be shared instead of our current milquetoast messaging.

The GOP has taken quite a hit from a public relations standpoint over the past decade, and frankly, we're not surprised. As a party we have to do better at branding. With outreach. With getting our message across in any and every medium that is humanly possible these days. We have to always be on our toes. And we simply have to hold ourselves to a different—and higher—standard. Because we're under a more intense microscope than the Left is, and as unfair as that may be, there's no sense in whining about it. It is what it is. We need to put on our big-girl panties and deal.

We're not suggesting for a second that we water down the message. No one needs to back down on principles or mindlessly accept whatever narrative the media wants to paint as the picture of conservatism. We're suggesting something completely different. Let's stop playing defense, and start creating our own narrative. Let's center it around the Constitution, limited government, and personal freedom—all the things that the Democrats suck at, frankly—and let's *package it better.*

We've entered a dimension where incredibly *suck* has become our new "not too bad." Where paying the yahoos in Congress $175,000 a year, while we work our keesters off to then watch them waste more of our money, is now the new norm. Where we're somehow expected to *respect* these folks for maybe-sorta-kinda thinking about *possibly* trying to get along to perhaps arrange a meeting to think about *considering* making a budget. Maybe. And we just accept it. And while we pay our taxes every year, give them more of our money, and listen to the narrative that we're fed, we just sit back and think, "Well, this is just the way it is."

It's not all doom and gloom. If it were, we wouldn't have quit our full-time day jobs to do this political thing. Let's face it. Our day jobs working for someone else offered a hell of a lot more stability; plus, we didn't get death threats from liberals. Ammo is *expensive*, y'all.

We believe in the American dream. We believe conservatism is right. And we believe that it's possible to spread those beliefs.

SO NOW WHAT? A GUIDE FOR INDIVIDUALS

If you've come this far with us, you may be asking yourself, "Well, what can *I* do?" People ask us that a lot. And our first response is usually, "Get involved locally." Whether it's with your local Tea Party or a local candidate's campaign, or your county's GOP chapter, that's a good start in political activism. In addition to those things, here's a list to get you started on the right path, because we Chicks dig lists:

1. **Talk to the young people in your life as much as you possibly can.** They're the future of this country, and they're inundated every single day by forces of liberal media. Those forces aren't on the conservative side of the spectrum, so *educate* them. Tell them what it means to be conservative. Give them this book, talk to them about the Constitution; then talk to them some more. Get involved *with* them, and cultivate civic duty in them at an early age. Schools are becoming indoctrination centers, so it's up to parents, aunts, uncles, older siblings—all of us—to make sure that we're promoting the message of conservatism at every opportunity to the kids in our lives.

2. **Stop being prudes.** If you're reading this and scolding us for using bad words or saying "OMG," stop it. If you're a conservative who's getting ready to send us an e-mail because one of the outfits we wore in a photo you saw of us on Facebook was too revealing for your taste, check yourself. *We are on the same freaking side.* So just *stop it*, and put your energies toward something useful, like a campaign or something. Seriously. You're a big part of the problem, if you haven't already realized it by now.

3. **Remember the 80/20 rule.** We subscribe to the idea of 80/20 conservatism that Ronald Reagan talked about. He knew human nature well enough to realize that people would never agree with him 100 percent of the time. He also recognized that someone who agreed with him 80 percent of the time was, in fact, an ally—not a 20 percent traitor. No candidate is perfect. No person is perfect. So stop looking for perfection. The only perfect person was Jesus Christ, and we don't see him running for office anytime soon. And if he did, the liberal media would crucify him. (No pun intended.)

4. **Stop with the labeling.** If someone calls his- or herself a Republican, and you call yourself a Republican, then chances are good that you'll agree about 80 percent of the time on issues. Embrace them, welcome them to the party, ask them if they'd like a beverage, and offer them a seat at the table. Seriously, didn't your mother teach you any manners? And we're not suggesting that you shouldn't call out misbehavior. We're not suggesting that there are, in fact, no RINOs. There are. But the RINO card is getting overplayed nearly as much as the race card is at this point. *Enough.* Let's focus more on our areas of agreement, and stop trying to demand carbon copies of ourselves.

A GUIDE FOR THE GOP

As important as it is for individual conservatives to take action, we think it is even more important that GOP leadership steps up and presents uncompromising conservative beliefs in much sexier packaging while also being much more aggressive about pummeling the crap out of liberal messaging. Here are some of our ideas:

1. **Stop playing defense, and start playing offense with our messaging.** It seems as though we're always a few steps behind the Left when it comes to communicating our message to the masses. Because the media is controlled almost exclusively by liberals (with the exception of Fox), we have to be proactive—rather than reactive—when it comes to getting our voice heard. Right now the media tells our story, and we have to defend ourselves. Instead, we need to tell people what our message is before the Left does. And while we're at it, we should tell them what the Left's message is, too, and beat them at their own game.

2. **Center messaging on limited government, personal freedom, and the Constitution.** If we are playing offense with clear, concise principles centered on these conservative ideals—all the things that the Democrats suck at, frankly—and we package those principles in a way that is fresh and to the point, we will win every time. We do not need to water down the message.

3. **Keep the social issues on the back burner.** We don't elect representatives to be preachers. This is where we get into trouble. We elect them to represent. We don't look to our politicians to be our moral compass, nor should we. They're elected to legislate, and most of the time they're spending a lot of our hard-earned money not doing *that* very well. So, when we hear our GOP representatives getting preachy, talking more about morality and social issues than about fiscal responsibility, we get our feathers a bit ruffled. Not only is it not their main job, but one misstep and liberals will pounce on those politicians and use them to paint *all* conservatives as intolerant, gay-hating bigots.

Stray comments from GOP politicians can do immeasurable damage to messaging, distracting from the main problems. We need to focus on the principles on which this country was founded, as much as humanly possible. If we do that, we'll continue to make strides in the right direction.

4. **Encourage, embrace, and empower women and minorities to run for office on the Republican ticket.** We know that there are amazing women and minorities in the GOP, but the Left has done a bang-up job making everyone think otherwise. We need to highlight the success stories within our party as much as possible (using guideline number 1), encouraging *more* of these folks to become involved in conservative politics until their presence becomes the norm, not the exception. That doesn't mean we should pander to key demographics that we're currently losing. It means we should include them in the conversation and feature them as examples of what GOP success looks like. As of this writing, there are four Republican female governors, compared to one Democrat. The only black U.S. senator is a Republican. Theirs are the stories we need to share.

5. **Be the party of straight talk—something we don't often see in today's political landscape.** People respond to straight talk that is relevant and delivered in a conversational tone—in fact, people on the right are downright hungry for that kind of communication. Regular people don't want to hear about sequesters and filibusters and whatever other buzzwords are floating around the media. They want to hear about how their kids' schools are going to improve, how they're going to get their next job, when gas prices will go down, and what kind of tax break they're going to get next year. They want to hear how the GOP can help this country in terms that are meaningful to them

specifically. They want to hear about tangible solutions that will help them as individuals—who, by the way, come in all shapes, sizes, and colors and from different backgrounds and varying circumstances. Conservatives don't want to hear a bunch of circular talk from a bunch of old white dudes on a faraway, out-of-touch Hill. They want to hear from people who can relate to them, who understand their day-to-day issues, and who can help them find real solutions. We need to tell the truth, cut through the crap, political correctness be damned.

6. **Remember we are human beings—not drones.** When planning events or meetings for constituents, the GOP really needs to loosen the freak *up.* Take off the seersucker and the ties. Laugh more. Live a little. Take the plug out of our keesters and choose barbeque and beer over chicken marsala and pinot noir. Relax. Conservatives need to let loose and be real, for crying out loud. We're not all walking around with sticks up our backsides, so why is it that we have to sound so much like buttoned-up, pretentious know-it-alls to get our message across? We don't. And people respond to other real people. It's time for us to ditch the messaging suited for a khakis-and-blazers crowd and tailor it for real people with real problems, offering them solutions that can make their lives better—in a way that a trustworthy friend would do it in a one-on-one conversation.

7. **Work every facet of media that Democrats do—and do it better.** Use pop culture. Use social media. Use celebrities. As much as we hate to say it, politicians need to go on talk shows, go on *Saturday Night Live,* get on "Between Two Ferns," and help the American public understand that they are human beings rather than one-dimensional politicians. We need to be posting like crazy on YouTube, with strong background

music and forceful messaging. We need to be all over TV, giving facts and data not with whining and handwringing but with forceful, aggressive flair. We need the GOP to explain in very clear terms (with a mix of snark and humor so it appeals to the younger generations) what we're all about. We need to create television shows that carefully and thoughtfully promote a conservative message. We need to develop kick-ass musical talents who don't necessarily sing *about* conservatism and make it all obvious (and therefore unappealing), but who write catchy, hip tunes which have understated conservative *themes*. We need to create talk shows like *The View* or *Ellen*, led by female and gay *conservatives*, which appeal to people in the same way that those shows already do. In other words, we need to realize that America has been dumbed down by liberalism, and we need to bring the level of discussion down to the lowest common denominator—the Obama voter. We might find it distasteful, and we might wrinkle our noses at the methods, but *that is what must be done*. We are in an age where politicians win in a popularity contest, more so than a competency contest, so it's time for us to adapt and step up. We might hate the game, but we've still got to play it in order to win.

8. **Quit recycling candidates.** And while we're figuring out how to play the game, let's quit using Ronald Reagan as an example of why it's acceptable to recycle candidates. Reagan ran in a different, social-media-free, and twenty-four-hour-news-cycle-free zone. Apples and oranges. People need fresh faces. People want new and improved. People don't want their dad's Republican Party, full of old white dudes. They want something *new*, which is why we're losing elections. The liberal media machine tarnishes and trashes candidates of yesteryear, so that by the time the next election cycle comes around,

they are damaged goods. It sucks, but it's the truth. We should be recruiting new potential candidates the way college sports teams do—by scouting out "young guns," grooming them early, and supporting them as they make their way through the political process.

9. **Fight fire with fire.** Responding to attacks with politeness hasn't gotten us anywhere. We need more pit bull and less Pomeranian. (No offense to either breed, but you know what we mean.) We need more feistiness. More spunk. More people unafraid of offending, and just determined to *tell it like it is*. We need to stop sitting back and being nicey nice and polite. We need to fight back against those who insist on trying to mold us into being kinder, gentler conservatives. Pardon our language, but *f*ck that*. We should *not* sit back while liberals beautifully weave together a story that craftily cuts down conservatives. Nope. Not on our watch.

We know that the Grand Ol' Party leaders probably won't read this book and immediately change their ways because of two chicks from Indiana. Like you, we are blips on the radar screen, because we don't always toe the establishment party line. We are normal, everyday people with everyday problems, without some sort of underlying agenda, much to the dismay of liberals who believe that we're paid Karl Rove or Koch brother operatives. (We still often check our mailboxes for those checks, though, just in case.) Not the kind of people that the establishment listens to.

Here's what we know for sure. We know that conservatives are not lemmings. They're not just going to follow the crowd. They're going to ask questions, and then *contemplate* responses, and then think some more. And unfortunately, what we've seen a lot of lately is that if they don't agree with even a portion of what is being dished out to them, some of them are simply tuning out. We cannot afford to let that happen, and it's time for the GOP to start making some changes to prevent this.

FEAR NOT, WEARY CONSERVATIVES!

But we won't despair even if there is no immediate response from Republican politicians. Instead, we are hopeful. We are hopeful because of the messages we get from supporters who tell us to persevere because we're resonating with them, and we're making a difference. The conservative makeover will succeed because there are people out there, just like us, who see this amazing country of ours on a downward spiral of sucktastic mediocrity and who are bound and determined to do something about it—come hell or high water.

Because that's the American spirit, y'all. And conservatives have it in spades.

It's a good thing we conservatives do have spirit, since many of us are exhausted. We're exhausted from being let down by the GOP, from being beat up by the liberal media, and from fighting with each other.

It's time for us to do what conservatives do best. Pick ourselves up, brush ourselves off, put our big-girl panties on, and get back in the game. And the good news? We're all in this together.

CONSERVATISM IS RIGHT. FOR ALL THE RIGHT REASONS.

There's an adage that goes, "Remember why you started." It's really easy for us to remember why we started Chicks on the Right with zero dollars down and a dream for something *better* for the future of this country. It's easy for us to remember why we continue to work our butts off to give conservatism a makeover. Because those reasons are ones we've created by God's grace, and they'll inherit this country long after we Chicks have left this earth (and the president definitely can't say we didn't build *them*).

The ultimate reasons behind every single thing that we Chicks do are the people who call us Mom.

But we do it for the people who call *you* Mom and Dad, or Aunt or Uncle or teacher, too. When we see *our* kids, we see *your* kids. We see our *country's* kids. And if there's one thing we Chicks have a soft spot about, it's the future of our nation's children.

We have five kids between the two of us—Amy Jo has three, and Miriam has two—and without them, we aren't sure how involved politically we might've been. It's their futures that drive us. It's a visceral need to make sure we're leaving behind a country that's as amazing and fruitful and exceptional as the one our parents and grandparents have left behind for us. Kids change the landscape, and if you're a parent, stepparent, grandparent, godparent, or just a really kick-ass aunt, uncle, teacher, or camp counselor, you get that. Our kids have, without question, served as fuel for our fire for the past five years, and that fire just grows hotter when we see things like each one of them already owing almost $60,000 in national debt for doing nothing but being born in the (once) free republic known as the United States of America. It's easy to get protective of our kids when we remember what it was like to grow up in Reagan's America, and we look into their big, trusting, the-world-is-my-oyster eyes. Our hearts literally break that they may not ever know the kind of America that we used to know.

Conservatism is right. And it's easy for us to fight for it every single day. It's like breathing to us now. Because it's simply the right ideology for a strong, resilient, thriving, *free* America. The kind of America that we used to know—the kind that we hope our children will one day be able to know.

Remember why America started, y'all.

We hold these Truths to be self-evident, that all Men are created equal, that they are endowed by their Creator with certain unalienable Rights, that among these are Life, Liberty and the pursuit of Happiness.

We're right. For all the right reasons.

TOGETHER, AMY JO AND MIRIAM EXTEND THEIR MOST HEARTFELT THANKS TO:

Maura Teitelbaum, literary agent extraordinaire, who believed that two complete dorks like us could write a book and have it get picked up by a major publishing house. Without her unwavering confidence and faith in us, this book never would have been written, let alone published by Sentinel.

Bria Sandford, Niki Papadopoulos, and the entire Sentinel team at Penguin Random House for their endless support and cheerleading (and shared adoration of Governor Mitch Daniels).

Governor Mitch Daniels, for taking an interest in two regular chicks who didn't know anything about anything, and making us feel important and valuable and heard. It's both a blessing and a curse that he was the first political rock star we met in person, because he set the bar impossibly high, and no one has come close to reaching it since.

Big E and Agent J, who were truly the first people to expose us in a real way to the World of Politics, and who've been genuinely delighted to watch us grow. We're so fortunate that a chance meeting at Indy's first Tea Party led to a lifelong friendship with two of the best people we know.

Andy Barnhart, for being our part-time webmaster, part-time bodyguard, and full-time friend. There's no one who could ever match his level of dedication and determination to help us be successful. And because of the serendipitous way we all found each other, we will now forever look at the death threat from a crazy-dude-in-his-mom's-basement with fondness.

David Wood, program director at WIBC, who took a major chance on two crazy chicks, plucked us out of our day jobs, and even though we didn't have a lick of radio experience, put us on the air during drive-time in Indianapolis. We will never be able to thank him enough for his belief in us, and his tutelage in a field where we're two absolute newbies. Plus, we love that he's secure enough in his masculinity to own the leopard shoe chair.

Matt Bair, our dear producer at WIBC, for putting up with so much estrogen on a daily basis, for getting us unsolicited sustenance when we were too busy to realize we even needed it, and for making us craugh (cry-laugh) on days when we didn't think we had laughter in us. He is an angel. We're convinced of it. (JANG SONG THAEK!)

Todd Starnes, for giving us Chicks an unexpected boost of publicity in January 2013 during The Great Facebook Shutdown Threat, for making us feel incredibly important with a personal tour of the Fox News headquarters in NYC, and for delighting us with his southern sweet-tea charm. Wednesdays wouldn't be the same without him.

Our clever and competent readers, who have been with us since the beginning. They are the somebodies who believed in two nobodies and for reasons that we'll never quite comprehend, became steadfast, loyal followers and friends in our crazy little community that is Chicks on the Right. We would be precisely nowhere without them, as they are the fuel for our fire, and they are ultimately the people who gave us the courage to even ponder the thought, "Hey . . . maybe we could write a book."

To the men and women who serve and have served our country, we are forever grateful. Without your sacrifices, we wouldn't have the ability to speak freely, pursue our dreams, and live in the most exceptional country on the planet. Freedom isn't free, and we never take what you've paid for our freedom for granted.

AMY JO'S ACKNOWLEDGMENTS

I would like to thank a thousand people, but for the sake of word count, here is my list of top thankees:

To God—you require no introduction, and you know why you're being thanked.

To Miri—I've always wanted to be a Charlie's Angel, and being a full-time Chick with her is pretty much as close as I'm going to get—without the cool hair or the bellbottoms or the Charlie. When she's in the room, the forecast is infinitely more Technicolor. I am thankful for her eternal optimism, even if I occasionally want to punch it in the face early in the morning before I've finished my coffee. I'm thankful that she's stood by me in giving a middle finger to "them" when they told us to be something other than *us*, because changing who we are would somehow make us more successful. At the end of the day, success is awesome, but if you don't have your sense of self— and if you don't have your friends? You don't have crap. So above all else, I'm thankful that you're my friend, Miri. What a ride it's been, and I'm so blessed that it's been with you.

To Greg, my best friend and love of my life—I don't think he realized the tornado of crazy he was taking on when he asked me to be his bride. It's a tight ship in our household, and Greg is the captain who holds it all together. While I've been pursuing my dream as a full-time Chick on the Right with some really wack hours, he's been cooking dinners, driving carpools, braiding hair, playing Barbies, cheering our daughter on at swimming and soccer, while also tending to our older children's needs. And he's still managed to buy me fresh flowers every payday and on many a morning, I miraculously have a cup of hot coffee in my hands to start my day. He does this with kisses, hugs, and with unabashed love in his heart, and he still manages to win at his own incredibly demanding career. He's never told me what to do, what to think, or how to act. He's never tried to change me. He's never even asked me to use that thing called a kitchen. He's just challenged me when I needed it, provided me with advice when I asked for it, and he has given me a home environment where I am safe and happy and—most important—loved without condition. For all of that, I'm thankful and sometimes in awe of his commitment to our life together, because I'm a freaking handful. *TTH, babe.*

To my Gweneth Paige, my heart and soul, my miracle, muse and legacy. She's too young to understand why my eyes were bloodshot and why I yawned so much back in 2014, but one day, I hope she will embrace the foundation of this book and understand me more as a woman who is fighting for something, in addition to my role as her mom. When I need to remind myself why I started, all I have to do is look at her face full of everything perfect in the world, and my batteries are instantly recharged. Because I definitely built *that*, Mr. President. And I will never, *ever* stop fighting for her.

To my mom, Alice, who simply forgot to say the words "you can't" throughout my life. Instead, she expected my inevitable success with the caveat that I worked my ass off to achieve it.

She never asked questions, even when I was engaging in paths to said success that involved walking on hot coals and playing with sharp knives. In her avoidance of those two words, I was once too naïve, and then I evolved into being too strong-willed, to know any better. And that has made all the difference. I thank her for being the most influential female role model in my life who has shown me that as a woman, it's important to live in the moment, but a chick always has to have a backup plan, be able to stand on her own two feet, and have the means to take care of herself—especially if she's going to be expected to take care of others.

To my mother-in-law, Nancy, who has provided countless hours of free child care, love, support, and home cooking (God knows I only have a kitchen because it came with my house). She's shown me, by example, that a woman can be placed in the most helpless of circumstances, left to raise a child on her own, and turn that situation around gracefully with absolutely zero handouts. And that child—with the right love, motivation, and steadfast dedication—can grow up to be the most amazing father and husband, even though he didn't have a father present in his upbringing. Because strong, conservative women are exceptional that way.

To my dad, Joe, who told me that if I was going to get an undergraduate degree and any parental assistance with said degree, I better come out with a tangible skill with that piece of paper. So I chose writing. I am thankful to him for forcing my hand in that choice. After writing countless things over the past twenty-plus years for other people, who got to write acknowledgments of *their* own? Well, here I am.

To my sister, Angie, who has always been my biggest cheerleader, my second mom, and a stream of endless giggling during every stage of my existence. I thank her for showing me, from birth, how absolutely, positively crucial women are in other women's lives.

To Carolyn Riley Kirk, my lifelong friend and confidante, thanks for answering my texts and phone calls when I needed to check in and vent and just have her hold my virtual hand over the past several decades, even when she had only thirty minutes to get ready for a fancy event as a proper military wife. Because no matter where life takes us, I know you'll always be there, and we're always going to be those painfully goofy eighteen-year-old sorority girls with some huge University of Tennessee hair. I simply won the friend lottery when I met you twenty-five years ago.

To Chase—who has stepped in countless times to selflessly tend to canines and chickens and a stray cat and a baby sister when we needed help over the past few years of craziness—despite his own teenage and college schedule. He's never wavered in his support of his wicked stepmonster and the Chickdom. *I thank you most for always having my back, kid. You are the shiznit.*

To Alyssa—who inadvertently teaches me about forgiveness every day. It's a necessity in this business, and it's one of the toughest things I've ever had to grasp.

MIRIAM'S ACKNOWLEDGMENTS

There are endless lists of people to whom I owe heartfelt thanks and sincere gratitude, but none so much as these:

Amy Jo—because HELLO. Without Amy Jo there would be no Chicks on the Right. And without Amy Jo my world would be infinitely less interesting. I've always believed she's the yin to my yang, the peas to my carrots, the peanut butter to my chocolate, and the rainbow to my skittles. She challenges me in all the right ways, and lets me have control when I need to be a freak about it. Her partnership goes far beyond our website and our radio gig and this book and COTR in general. It genuinely hurts my heart to know that there are people in the world who will never know what it means to have the kind of best friend that she is to me. AJ, I love you with the fury of a billion suns. And Ho Hos, bitches. And whatnot.

Ron—my sweet husband whom I fear I will never entirely deserve, for his exquisite, innate understanding of women and for shouldering an absurd amount of responsibility with endless patience, tolerance, and tenderness. I've often said that he should teach a How-To-Be-An-Awesome-Husband class, and I have his parents, Ron Sr. and Carole, to thank for raising him right. He's always indulged my every request, spoiling me rotten, and taking care of the homestead so I can be a Chick on the Right. He is forever where my heart is. Plus, he's really foxy. Honey—you are my world. Thank you for being exactly, perfectly you.

Thomas—my older son, for showing me and so many others what pure, unbridled joy looks like. His smile has claimed more hearts than I can count, and he is an accidental, unintentional teacher of some of life's most important lessons. The moment I allow myself the indulgence of self-pity, for any reason, I need only look at how he manages to brighten a room with his squeals of delight, despite the pain he endures daily, to remember that as an able-bodied, healthy person, I need to put my big-girl panties on and deal. There is no better motivation to persevere than beautiful, cheerful, magnificent Thomas.

Jackson—my remarkable, brilliant, charming "Boobaloo," for being so easy to love, and so easy to parent. The extent to which I simply am unable to empathize with typical mom struggles because of his exceptional goodness is almost embarrassing. *Almost.* Boo—you will never be able to fully appreciate how amazing it is for me to be your mom. There is nothing that gives me bigger warm and fuzzies than your deliciously goofy grin, and I hope someday you are lucky enough to have a kid as awesome as you are.

The Birds—my parents, whom I admire and look up to more than any other humans on the planet, for their endless sacrifices and selflessness. I can't imagine two better people from whom to inherit genetic code. Daddio—thank you for being the kind of parent it's fun to brag about having. Thank you for awesome childhood memories of badminton and playing cards, and for passing the relaxation gene down to me. (I probably have a mutated version of it though, because I do it to a fault.) Ma—you should be sainted. For real. There is no way to properly thank you for all that you do, and all that you give, and all that you are. Love you both so very much.

Danielle—my sister, for making me laugh like no one else can, for always knowing the correct answer to the question "Can I be mean for a second?," and for being the perfect sibling for me. Span—thank you for all of the glorious sister-time, and for being a willing suitcase dweller and coin-eater. BALLS BALLS BALLS.

Jamie—my sibling-by-choice, for being an indispensable part of my family forever, and for being Thomas' best friend in the whole wide world. Jamie—I cannot imagine our lives without you.

Buckeye Bob—for always being so fiercely protective of me and for delivering countless giggles to me and everyone else at TMD. I'm certain he is now my guardian angel. BB—I miss you every time I see anything inappropriate (which is a lot).

NOTES

CHAPTER 1: **Capitalism Is a Good Thing**

1. "The American People's New Economic Charter," *Wikispaces*, 9/30/11 .http://tapnec.wikispaces.com/.
2. Julie Shapiro, "Cafe Laid Off 21 Workers Because of Occupy Wall Street, Owner Says," *DNAinfo.com* New York, 11/1/2011 http://www.dnainfo .com/new-york/20111101/downtown/financial-district-cafe-lays-off-21-workers-because-of-occupy-wall-street.
3. Jeff Gordinier, "Want to Get Fat on Wall Street? Try Protesting," *New York Times*, 10/11/11, http://www.nytimes.com/2011/10/12/dining/protesters-at-occupy-wall-street-eat well.html?_r=3&.
4. Robert Rector, "Obama's New 'Poverty' Measurement," *National Review Online* 3/1/10, http://www.nationalreview.com/articles/229274/obamas-new-poverty-measurement/robert-rector.
5. Robert Rector and Rebecca Sheffield, "Obama's New Poverty Measure 'Spreads the Wealth,'" The Heritage Foundation, 11/9/11, http://www.heritage.org/research/commentary/2011/11/obamas-new-poverty-measure-spreads-the-wealth.
6. Diane Rado, "Honors class leads to diversity debate," *Chicago Tribune*, 11/23/10, http://articles.chicagotribune.com/2010-11-23/news/ct-met-detracking-20101123_1_english-class-diversity-debate-rigorous-classes.
7. Stanislas Jourdan, "Lessons from Mincome: How a Basic Income Would Improve Health," Basic Income UK, 8/7/13, http://basicincome.org.uk/interview/2013/08/health-forget-mincome-poverty/.
8. Erica Ritz, "President Obama: 'If You've Got a Business—You Didn't Build That. Somebody Else Made That Happen,'" The Blaze, 7/14/12, http://www .theblaze.com/stories/2012/07/14/president-obama-if-youve-got-a-business-you-didnt-build-that-somebody-else-made-that-happen/.

CHAPTER 2: **America Is Exceptional**

1. "Polls: Is America Exceptional?" CNN, 9/12/13 http://politicalticker.blogs.cnn.com/2013/09/12/polls-is-america-exceptional/.

2. Matt Wilstein, "Bill Maher and Guests Rail Against 'Complacent and Smug' American Exceptionalism," Mediaite, 3/14/14. http://www.mediaite.com/tv/bill-maher-and-guests-rail-against-complacent-and-smug-american-exceptionalism/.

3. Congressional Record, "JOINT MEETING TO HEAR AN ADDRESS BY HIS EXCELLENCY FELIPE CALDERON HINOJOSA, PRESIDENT OF MEXICO" Library of Congress, 5/20/10 http://thomas.gov/cgi-bin/query/z?r111:H20MY0-0010.

4. Jon Huey," 'E Pluribus Unum'—A Response to President Calderon," Tommcclintock.com, 5/20/10 http://www.tommcclintock.com/blog/e-pluribus-unum-a-response-to-president-calderon.

5. Pew Research Center,"Second-Generation Americans: A Portrait of the Adult Children of Immigrants," Pew Research Center, 2/7/13 http://www.pewsocialtrends.org/files/2013/02/FINAL_immigrant_generations_report_2-7-13.pdf.

CHAPTER 3: **Hand Ups, Not Handouts**

1. Joey Horta, "Exclusive: $7,000+ Food Stamp Balance," Valleycentral.com, 2/20/13 http://www.valleycentral.com/news/story.aspx?id=863400#.U0CYBKLhFJL.

2. Katherine Mangu-Ward, "The Giving Gap," Reason.com, 12/19/06 http://reason.com/archives/2006/12/19/the-giving-gap.

3. Nicholas Kristof, "Bleeding Heart Tightwads," *New York Times,* 12/20/08 http://www.nytimes.com/2008/12/21/opinion/21kristof.html?_r=0.

4. Scott Shane, "Balancing Economic Control and Entrepreneurship," Smallbiztrends.com, 12/10/12, http://smallbiztrends.com/2012/12/balancing-economic-control-and-entrepreneurship.html?extlink=dw-openf-original-source.

5. Nicholas Kristof, "Profiting From A Child's Illiteracy," *New York Times,* 12/09/12 http://www.nytimes.com/2012/12/09/opinion/sunday/kristof-profiting-from-a-childs-illiteracy.html?pagewanted=all&_r=1&.

CHAPTER 4: **First Amendment Protections Extend to All Americans, Not Just Those with Whom We Agree**

1. Kevin Hassett, "Commencement Speakers: Conservatives Need Not Apply," *Miami Herald,* 5/26/13 http://www.miamiherald.com/2013/05/26/3414349/commencement-speakers-conservatives.html#storylink=cpy.

2. Tal Kopan, "Student stopped from handing out Constitutions on Constitution Day sues," Politico, 10/10/13, http://www.politico.com/blogs/under-the-radar/2013/10/student-stopped-from-handing-out-constitutions-on-174792.html.

3. Paul Elias, "Court: School can ban US flag shirts for safety," Associated Press, 2/27/14 http://bigstory.ap.org/article/court-school-can-ban-us-flag-shirts-safety.

4. Ibid.
5. "California college student teaches school $50,000 lesson on Constitution," Foxnews.com, 2/25/14 http://www.foxnews.com/us/2014/02/25/california-college-student-teaches-school-50000-lesson-on-constitution/.
6. Noel Sheppard, "Kirsten Powers: Liberals Shun Opposing Views Because They're Used to Controlling the Media," Newsbusters.org, 1/23/13 http://newsbusters.org/blogs/noel-sheppard/2013/01/23/kirsten-powers-liberals-shun-opposing-views-because-theyre-used-contr#ixzz2sCXzYVfl.
7. Blake Yount, flag@whitehouse.gov asks Americans to send them sources of disinformation in the health care debate, Examiner.com, 8/4/09 http://www.examiner.com/article/flag-whitehouse-gov-asks-americans-to-send-them-sources-of-disinformation-the-health-care-debate.

CHAPTER 5: Political Correctness Is Stupid

1. David Masciotra, "Political correctness is about to get even worse on college campuses," *Indianapolis Star,* 6/12/13, http://www.indystar.com/apps/pbcs.dll/article?AID=/201306121848/OPINION13/306120051.
2. Edmund Demarche, "Pennsylvania girl, 5, suspended for threatening to shoot girl with pink toy gun that blows soapy bubbles," Fox News, 1/19/13. http://www.foxnews.com/us/2013/01/19/pennsylvania-girl-5-suspended-for-threatening-to-shoot-girl-with-pink-toy-gun/#ixzz2IR6JNHry.
3. Cristina Constantini, "Associated Press Drops 'Illegal Immigrant' From Stylebook," Fusion.net, 4/2/13. http://fusion.net/american_dream/story/press-drops-illegal-immigrant-standards-book-11194#.UVw_D6Lqlc1.
4. Bret Baier, "Terrorism Is a 'Man-Caused' Disaster?" Foxnews.com, 3/17/09 http://www.foxnews.com/story/2009/03/17/terrorism-is-man-caused-disaster/.
5. Michael Daly, "Nidal Hasan's Murders Termed Workplace Violence by US," Daily Beast, 8/8/13 http://www.thedailybeast.com/articles/2013/08/06/nidal-hasan-s-murders-termed-workplace-violence-by-u-s.html.
6. Maryland EBT Independence Card, https://www.ebt.acs-inc.com/ebtcard/mdebt/index.jsp.
7. David Masciotra, "Political Correctness is about to get even worse on college campuses," *Indianapolis Star,* 6/12/13, http://www.indystar.com/apps/pbcs.dll/article?AID=/201306121848/OPINION13/306120051.
8. "Fairytales too scary for modern children, say parents," The Telegraph, 2/12/12, http://www.telegraph.co.uk/news/newstopics/howaboutthat/9078489/Fairytales-too-scary-for-modern-children-say-parents.html.
9. Peter Glick and Susan Fiske, "Hostile and Benevolent Sexism: Measuring Ambivalent Sexist Attitudes Toward Women," *Psychology of Women Quarterly,* March, 2007, http://pwq.sagepub.com/content/21/1/119.
10. http://banbossy.com.
11. http://dictionary.reference.com/browse/bossy?s=t.
12. J. Bryan Lowder, "What Is a "Preferred Gender Pronoun," and Is It Always Obnoxious?" Slate.com, 7/10/13, http://www.slate.com/blogs/xx_factor/2013/07/10/preferred_gender_pronouns_what_are_they_and_is_the_practice_of_pgps_always.html.

13. "What the heck is a PGP?" Gay Straight Alliance for Safe Schools, http://www.gsafewi.org/wp-content/uploads/What-the-heck-is-a-PGP1.pdf.
14. http://www.r-word.org/.
15. http://www.thinkb4youspeak.com/.
16. James Harris, "New Terminology for Mental Retardation in DSM-5 and ICD-11,"medscape.com, 2013, http://www.medscape.com/viewarticle/782769.

CHAPTER 6: **We Have a Constitutional Right to Things That Go Pew-Pew-Pew**

1. Eric Owens, "Gun Stun: Gun control activist swears he forgot he was carrying gun while visiting school." The Daily Caller, May 15, 2014, http://dailycaller.com/2014/02/10/gun-stun-gun-control-activist-swears-he-forgot-he-was-carrying-gun-while-visiting-school.
2. Heather Mallick, "Why Newtown victim Noah Pozner had an open coffin." *Toronto Star,* Jan 22 2013, http://www.thestar.com/opinion/editorialopinion/2013/01/22/mallick_why_newtown_victim_noah_pozner_had_an_open_coffin.html.
3. "U.S. Abortion Rate Up Slightly After Years of Decline." Fox News, January 11, 2011, http://www.foxnews.com/health/2011/01/10/abortion-rate-stalls-years-decline/.
4. "Howard Stern Show : Harvey Weinstein Interview 01/15/14." https://www.youtube.com/watch?v=lig_yRICAro.
5. Erik Wemple, "Navy Yard Shooter: What about that alleged AR-15?" *Washington Post,* September 17, 2013, http://www.washingtonpost.com/blogs/erik-wemple/wp/2013/09/17/navy-yard-shooter-what-about-that-alleged-ar-15/.
6. Christopher Rosen, "Eddie Vedder On Gun Control Opponents: 'I Almost Wish Bad Things Upon These People'." *Huffington Post,* October 9, 2013, http://www.huffingtonpost.com/2013/10/09/eddie-vedder-gun-control_n_4059887.html?ncid=edlinkusaolp00000003.
7. Tom Watkins and Ana Cabrera, Ana Centennial, "Colorado's school shooting—over in 80 seconds." CNN, December 15, 2013, http://www.cnn.com/2013/12/14/us/colorado-school-shooting/.

CHAPTER 7: **Skin Color Is Irrelevant**

1. Julie Henry, "Dress witches in pink and avoid white paper to prevent racism in nurseries, expert says." *The Telegraph,* September 25, 2011, http://www.telegraph.co.uk/education/educationnews/8786641/Dress-witches-in-pink-and-avoid-white-paper-to-prevent-racism-in-nuseries-expert-says.html.
2. James Taranto, "Hot Enough For You?" The Wall Street Journal, February 22, 2010, http://online.wsj.com/news/articles/SB10001424052748703382904575059270348147154 (accessed May 15, 2014).
3. Katherine Kersten, "At U, future teachers may be reeducated." *Star Tribune,* December 2, 2009, http://www.startribune.com/opinion/70662162.html#VIJOj93qGjm4hilp.97.

4. Ibid.
5. Ibid.
6. Joe Newby, "Portland school sees racism in peanut butter and jelly sandwiches." Examiner.com, September 10, 2012. http://www.examiner.com/article/portland-school-sees-racism-peanut-butter-and-jelly-sandwiches.
7. Katherine Kersten, "Always room in the budget for white guilt." *Star Tribune,* April 9, 2011, http://www.startribune.com/opinion/commentaries/119508364.html.
8. Jeff Poor, "Walter E. Williams on welfare: As gov't plays 'father,' 'black males have become dispensable" The Daily Caller, June 4, 2011, http://dailycaller.com/2011/06/04/walter-e-williams-on-welfare-as-govt-plays-father-black-males-have-become-dispensable/#ixzz2wj90meoy.
9. Thomas Sowell, "Policies of left often hurt blacks." *The Columbus Dispatch.* October 6, 2011, http://www.dispatch.com/content/stories/editorials/2011/10/06/policies-of-left-often-hurt-blacks.html.
10. David A Clarke, Jr. "Liberal policies have destroyed the black family," Washington Times, March 24, 2014, http://p.washingtontimes.com/news/2014/mar/24/clarke-social-liberalism-the-new-racism/?page=all#pagebreak.
11. "Liberal policies harm black Americans." timesfreepress.com, July 28, 2013, http://www.timesfreepress.com/news/2013/jul/28/liberal-policies-harm-black-americans/.
12. David Horowitz and John Perazzo, "Government Versus the People: The Four Poorest American Cities." US Census Bureau, 2007, http://www.frontpagemag.com/upload/pamphlets/government-vs-the-people.pdf.
13. "Income, Poverty and Health Insurance Coverage in the United States: 2010." US Census Bureau, September 13, 2011, http://www.census.gov/newsroom/releases/archives/income_wealth/cb11-157.html.
14. Peter Kirsanow, "Blacks, Democrats, and Republicans." *National Review Online,* March 15, 2011, http://www.nationalreview.com/corner/262180/blacks-democrats-and-republicans-peter-kirsanow.
15. Dan Merica, "Blacks outvoted whites in 2012, the first time on record." CNN.com, May 9, 2013, http://politicalticker.blogs.cnn.com/2013/05/09/blacks-outvoted-whites-in-2012-the-first-time-on-record/.
16. Stephen Dinan, "Welfare spending jumps 32% during Obama's presidency." *Washington Times,* October 18, 2012, http://www.washingtontimes.com/news/2012/oct/18/welfare-spending-jumps-32-percent-four-years/?page=all.
17. Wayne Brough, "Six Years Later, Obama's Policies Still Aren't Creating Jobs." RealClearMarkets, March 13, 2014, http://www.realclearmarkets.com/articles/2014/03/13/six_years_later_obamas_policies_still_arent_creating_jobs_100953.html (accessed May 15, 2014).

CHAPTER 8: **The War on Women Is Crap**

1. Shushannah Walshe, "How Pissed Off Are Republican Women?" *Marie Claire,* July 18, 2012, http://www.marieclaire.com/world-reports/news/republican-party-women.

2. Erin Gloria Ryan, "Listen Up, Men: Here's How Romney's Views on Women Will Make Your Life More Difficult." *Jezebel,* October 22, 2012, http://jezebel.com/5953760/listen-up-men-how-romneys-views-on-women-will-make-your-life-more-difficult.

3. Laura Beck, "Student Mag Censored for Featuring 18 Different Vaginas on Cover [NSFW]." *Jezebel,* August 21, 2013, http://jezebel.com/student-mag-censored-for-featuring-18-different-vaginas-1180714520.

4. Ryan, Hannah, Avani Dias, Mariana Podesta-Diverio, and Lucy Watson. "Are vulvas so obscene that we have to censor them?" *The Guardian,* August 21, 2013, http://www.theguardian.com/commentisfree/2013/aug/22/honi-soit-vulvas-censorship.

5. "Analysis of New 2010 Census Poverty Data—September 2011." National Women's Law Center, September 22, 2011, http://www.nwlc.org/analysis-new-2010-census-poverty-data-%E2%80%93-september-2011.

6. Michael W. Chapman, "780,000 More Women Unemployed Today Than When Obama Took Office." CNS News, July 6, 2012, http://cnsnews.com/news/article/780000-more-women-unemployed-today-when-obama-took-office.

7. Erin Gloria Ryan, "Listen Up, Men: Here's How Romney's Views on Women Will Make Your Life More Difficult." *Jezebel,* October 22, 2012, http://jezebel.com/5953760/listen-up-men-how-romneys-views-on-women-will-make-your-life-more-difficult.

8. "The Life of Julia." Organizing for Action. http://l.barackobama.com/truth-team/entry/the-life-of-julia.

9. "Has 'The Life of Julia' ended already?" *The Daily Caller,* August 15, 2013, http://dailycaller.com/2013/10/15/has-the-life-of-julia-ended-already/.

10. Lindsey Burke and David B. Muhlhausen, PhD. "Head Start Impact Evaluation Report Finally Released." The Heritage Foundation, January 10, 2013, http://www.heritage.org/research/reports/2013/01/head-start-impact-evaluation-report-finally-released.

11. David Jesse, "Colleges chase Pell Grant scammers." *USA Today,* February 17, 2013, http://www.usatoday.com/story/news/nation/2013/02/16/colleges-chase-pell-grant-scammers/1925013.

12. Gentilviso, Chris. "Todd Akin Likens Claire McCaskill To 'One Of Those Dogs,' Fetching Taxes, Bureaucracy (AUDIO)." *Huffington Post,* October 21, 2012, http://www.huffingtonpost.com/2012/10/21/todd-akin-claire-mccaskill_n_1995088.html.

13. Bassett, Laura. "Todd Akin: Claire McCaskill Was Much More 'Ladylike' In 2006." *Huffington Post,* September 27, 2012, http://www.huffingtonpost.com/2012/09/27/todd-akin-claire-mccaskill_n_1920271.html.

CHAPTER 9: **We Are Pro-Life**

1. William Saletan, "Can Obama take the politics out of abortion?" *Slate Magazine,* October 16, 2008, http://www.slate.com/articles/health_and_science/human_nature/2008/10/safe_legal_and_boring.html.

2. "Barack Obama on Abortion." PoliGu.com, October 4, 2012, http://www.thepoliticalguide.com/Profiles/President/US/Barack_Obama/Views/Abortion/.

3. Daniel Doherty, "Is America Becoming a Pro-Life Nation?" townhall.com, July 10, 2013, http://townhall.com/tipsheet/danieldoherty/2013/07/10/is-america-becoming-a-more-prolife-nation-n1637706.

4. "Doctor Kermit Gosnell found guilty of murdering infants in late-term abortions." Foxnews.com, May 13, 2013, http://www.foxnews.com/us/2013/05/13/jury-split-on-2-counts-in-trial-abortion-doctor-kermit-gosnell/.

5. R. Seth Williams, "Report of the Grand Jury." First Judicial District of Pennsylvania Criminal Trial Division, January 14, 2011, http://www.phila.gov/districtattorney/pdfs/grandjurywomensmedical.pdf.

6. John McCormack, "Wendy Davis: 'I don't know what happened in the Gosnell case'" *The Weekly Standard*, August 5, 2013, https://www.weeklystandard.com/blogs/wendy-davis-i-dont-know-what-happened-gosnell-case_742625.html.

7. R. Seth Williams, "Report of the Grand Jury." First Judicial District of Pennsylvania Criminal Trial Division, January 14, 2011, http://www.phila.gov/districtattorney/pdfs/grandjurywomensmedical.pdf.

8. Mary Elizabeth Williams, "Is motherhood Natalie Portman's "greatest role"?" Salon.com, February 28, 2011. http://www.salon.com/2011/02/28/natalie_portman_most_important_role/.

9. Eric Wemplek, "Gosnell case: HuffPost host says left 'made a decision' to not cover trial." Washington Post, August 16, 2013, http://www.washingtonpost.com/blogs/erik-wemple/wp/2013/04/16/gosnell-case-huffpost-host-says-left-made-a-decision-to-not-cover-trial/.

10. "Abortions In America." Operation Rescue. http://www.operationrescue.org/about-abortion/abortions-in-america/ (This page is updated regularly).

11. Beth Merfish, "My Mother's Abortion." *New York Times,* July 7, 2013, http://www.nytimes.com/2013/07/08/opinion/my-mothers-abortion.html?_r=0.

12. Joel B. Pollack, "California's Brown Signs Bill Permitting Non-Physician Abortions." Breitbart News Network, October 9, 2013, http://www.breitbart.com/Big-Government/2013/10/09/California-s-Brown-Signs-Bill-Permitting-Non-Physician-Abortions.

CHAPTER 10: **We Are Pro-Contraception and Pro–Plan B**

1. "Plan B One-Step®: FAQs." Plan B One-Step®: FAQs. http://www.planbonestep.com/faqs.aspx.

2. http://sblog.s3.amazonaws.com/wp-content/uploads/2013/10/13-354-BRIEF-OF-AMICI-CURIAE-PHYSICIANS-FOR-REPRODUCTIVE-HEALTH-et-al. . . . pdf.

3. Karen Prior, "The Pill: Contraceptive or Abortifacient?" *The Atlantic*, December 31, 2012, http://www.theatlantic.com/sexes/archive/2012/12/the-pill-contraceptive-or-abortifacient/266725/.

4. WD Mosher and J Jones, "Use of Contraception in the United States: 1982–2008." National Center for Health Statistics Vital Health Stat, 23 (29), August 2010, http://www.cdc.gov/nchs/data/series/sr_23/sr23_029.pdf.

5. "Personhood," ProlifeWisconsin.com, http://www.prolifewisconsin.org/pro LifeIssues.asp?aid=399&article=Federal+Personhood+Legislation&id=7.
6. Kathleen Parker, "Prude or prudent? The debate over access to Plan B." *Washington Post*, May 3, 2013. http://www.washingtonpost.com/opinions/ kathleen-parker-plan-b-and-who-gets-to-decide-for-children/2013/05/03/ c88d3762-b418-11e2-9a98-4be1688d7d84_story.html.

CHAPTER 11: **We Don't Care Whom You Sleep With**

1. Tony Lee, "NBA Player Jason Collins Comes Out, Is First Active Gay Athlete in Major Sports." Breitbart News Network, April 29, 2013, http://www.breitbart.com/Breitbart-Sports/2013/04/29/Jason-Collins-Reveals-He-Is-Gay.
2. Tony Lee, "Michelle Tweets, Barack Calls Jason Collins After He Comes Out." Breitbart News Network, April 29, 2013, http://www.breitbart.com/ Breitbart-Sports/2013/04/29/Obamas-Tweet-Call-Jason-Collins.
3. "Our Message To Liberals," Gayconservative.org, http:// gayconserva tive.org.
4. Drew Magary, "Duck Dynasty's Phil Robertson Gives Drew Magary a Tour." *GQ*, January 2014, http://www.gq.com/entertainment/television/ 201401/duck-dynasty-phil-robertson.
5. Ross Murray, "Duck Dynasty's Phil Robertson uses vile stereotypes to tell GQ his thoughts on LGBT people." GLAAD.org, December 18, 2013, http://www.glaad.org/blog/duck-dynastys-phil-robertson-uses-vile-stereotypes-tell-gq-his-thoughts-lgbt-people.
6. Fred Lucas, "Court Says Christian Couple's Refusal to Photograph Same-Sex Ceremony Was Illegal—Why 'You Will Be Made to Care'." The Blaze. com, August 23, 2013, http://www.theblaze.com/stories/2013/08/23/court-says-christian-couples-refusal-to-photograph-same-sex-ceremony-was-illegal-why-you-will-be-made-to-care/.
7. "85% Think Christian Photographer Has Right to Turn Down Same-Sex Wedding Job," Rasmussen Reports,7/12/13 http://www.rasmussenreports .com/public_content/business/general_business/july_2013/85_think_ christian_photographer_has_right_to_turn_down_same_sex_wedding_job.

INDEX

209